TRANSFORMATION

A WOMEN WHO SUBMIT ANTHOLOGY

MANAGING EDITORS
Ryane Nicole Granados
Noriko Nakada

FICTION EDITORS
Lorinda Toledo
Erin Anadkat

CREATIVE NONFICTION EDITORS
Flint
Laura Sturza

POETRY EDITORS
Luivette Resto
Aruni Wijesinghe
Hazel Kight Witham

DRAMA EDITOR
Lucy Rodriguez-Hanley

ADVISING EDITOR
Tisha Marie Reichle-Aguilera, PhD

Transformation: A Women Who Submit Anthology

Jamii Publishing

Jamii Publishing
Santa Cruz, CA
www.jamiipublishing.com
[clmp]

Front Cover Design: Rachael Warecki

Managing Editors: Ryane Nicole Granados and Noriko Nakada

Copy Editor: Xochitl-Julisa Bermejo

Production: Nikia Chaney, Cynthia Manick, Emily Blair

ISBN: 978-1-954901-91-9

Given these perilous times of great global and local humanitarian failures, cruel objectives cemented by morally repugnant mindsets, and given the history of violence which has proven all too predictable, I know my words may appear hugely insufficient in protecting the most vulnerable, may prove never to be enough to diminish the sorrow and suffering of others, and yet as a writer, I continue to write.

Helena María Viramontes, writer of fiction,
an elder, a teacher, and a Chicana feminist

Keynote Address AWP 2020

ACKNOWLEDGEMENTS

This anthology was made possible by a grant from California Arts Council, sponsorship by Antioch University Los Angeles, the generosity of individual donors, and the fiscal sponsorship of Avenue 50 Studio.

This publication could not exist without the collaboration of Nikia Chaney at Jamii Publishing.

We are also grateful for the mentorship and ongoing support of Sarah Rafael Garcia at LibroMobile.

And many heartfelt thank yous to Rachael Warecki who designs our beautiful covers and continues to offer informal technical support throughout the editorial process.

Thank you to all the chapter leads across the globe who continue to gather and support the submission efforts of our members.

TRANSFORMATION was inspired by Helena María Viramontes's keynote address at AWP 2020 in San Antonio. It is our hope that this collection of work will speak to ways writers and other artists can promote change in the world.

Women Who Submit was created in response to the 2010 VIDA Count. We are grateful to VIDA: Women in Literary Arts for their inspiration and commitment to creating transparency around the lack of gender parity in the literary landscape and to amplifying historically-marginalized voices, including people of color; writers with disabilities; and queer, trans and gender nonconforming individuals. (www.vidaweb.org)

CONTENTS

CREATIVE NONFICTION

POETRY

Foreword

by NORIKO NAKADA and RYANE NICOLE GRANADOS

It all started with an ask from our advising editor, Tisha Marie Reichle-Aguilera.

"Ryane, Noriko, I think you two should be managing editors for the next Women Who Submit anthology."

Crickets. I'm pretty sure that's what Tisha heard from us on the other end, mostly because we are both mothers, working mothers, who, despite Tisha's belief, felt unsure we could take on ONE. MORE. THING. in all of the things we do in our lives. That has been Tisha's role for both of us within Women Who Submit: seeing something in us that we didn't see ourselves.

Five years ago, Tisha tapped us both for Women Who Submit's leadership team. At that point, we were active members. We had hosted submission parties at our homes and reaped the benefits of Women Who Submit's mission to empower women and non-binary writers to submit our work for publication. We had already learned about the editorial process for WWS anthologies as creative nonfiction genre editors for ACCOLADES, and by mentoring fiction and creative nonfiction editors for GATHERING. But this? Managing editors? That was Tisha's job. She guided us through that process with both ACCOLADES and GATHERING. Now she was asking us to make a book, with calls for submissions and curating, and guiding other editors through the process. There would be covers and tables of contents and in the end a book was expected to bloom. How could such busy people take this on? How?

And yet, here we are, and on the other end of that ask is indeed an actual book with another gorgeous cover designed by

Rachel Warecki. We stand on the shoulders of our advising editor and our incredible team of genre editors with this powerful collection of words. We are transformed again, from writers, to editors, to managing editors.

That is the power of transformation that Women Who Submit pushes. We transform ourselves from private writers, penning poems and essays, stories and plays in our notebooks and on our laptops, and then we go public. With the simple ask, to push our words into the world, we change it. We change the publishing industry one submission at a time, one book at a time, and the organization changes the way artists and creatives support one another. Rather than seeing other writers as competition in a climate of scarcity, we see one another as resources and mentors. In Women Who Submit, we see how others have done things, we bear witness to the planting of seeds, we come together to water those seeds, and in doing so we remove the veil of the publishing process, recognizing it isn't some magical act, but when done in community it can be a beautiful one. It can transform a lifeless landscape into a garden, filled with vibrant words ready for the reader to harvest.

We are excited to welcome you into that harvest. We are thrilled to have you read lines of prose and poetry that made us gasp. We invite you to imagine our poetry editors pushing through what is always a very arduous process due to multi-submissions being made by our community of poets. We ask you to bear witness to the difficult decisions the creative nonfiction editors had to make as they worked to create equitable space in the book for other pages. We implore you to envision our fiction editors engaging in effective mentorship from one previous editor to a new WWS anthology editor. And we welcome you to celebrate with our drama editor who fielded more submissions in drama than we ever had, thereby highlighting the significance of the work we do in the literary landscape.

Enjoy the view!

TRANSFORMATION

Care Instructions for a Colored Girl

by .CHISARAOKWU.

from Hennepin Review

who is fatherless

who searches for mother
in lovers but can't find pussy
hard enough to climb

who catches love
with her teeth
knots it with tongue
swallows hard

who stomachs the rape
cheats death

who baskets summer
fruit too ripe
too bruised to eat
too love full

who still wrings her skin
of wet between her legs

who cries for help again & again
& again— no one comes
no one comes

:

don't pretend to be her daddy.

don't ask her where she came from.
don't ask her nothing.

add her to your love cycle.
every Tuesday.

comb her hair. listen to everything

she cannot whisper. write it down.
tell her you love her
hands.

clean her wounds with dead sea
water. ask her what hurts.
butterfly kiss her cheeks.
purple her path
with lavender & lilac.
leave gauze for her to wipe with.

note the color
of her yes. let it be so.
let her be
her own gift.
the muthafucking prize.

don't hang her out to dry.

believe her. give
ice for her tongue.
a night light for dreams.
space to spill
brokenwholeheartsong
wherever she choses.

ask her what her
name is.
if she tells you
praise this gift

Madwoman

after Lucille Clifton

by .CHISARAOKWU.

i.

they say I'm cursed for longing
I mean I   know
I am feetstuck
between riverstones
coveting wet rage
coldwait for you
I mean you
are always in the river
that I must cross
meaning I
am not swimming this   I mean I
am narcissus chasing eyelashes
down the winding
slipping on rocks
bearded with blue moss
I mean they
can't detangle the wet knot of fingers
gripping my matted hair
I really mean they
deranged entanglements of ripped skin
dead cells   misfiring neurons
depleted cellular scaffold   a flood of black
eyes darting leftrightleftrightleft
what a fright

we are
the whole lot of us
seeking home
in the river's white face

ii.
I that eyes
the body that I inhabits
            I that mimics
the world in search of itself
I that does not multitude   but I
—booted & strapped— eyes multitudes
of documents, records, identities
sewn to the body as body's validity
yet here   & always   the I that wings
its fangs in search of salvo
that winks upon this bodymap
I shudder because I find myself
capitulating to I, I demanding
everything for nothing
as it were millennia ago
as it were today beneath a cloud
I search safe
eyes look back

Bhangra

by ANITA GILL

from The Offing

As laughter echoed in the lobby of the Katzen Arts Center, I began to ponder collective nouns. If a group of crows is a murder and a group of owls is a parliament, what would the term be for a group of undergraduates? No word came to mind, so I christened the gathered American University students a "headache." And this headache intensified my anxiety about trying out for the school's Bhangra team. Dance wasn't my strong suit, but I believed my Punjabi background was a latent superpower I was about to uncover.

I crept over to the lobby wall, all the while never taking my eyes off the youths. The shorts, yoga pants, and sports bra straps peeking out of cotton shirts made me self-conscious in my khakis and button-down shirt. At 24 years old, I was probably not the ideal candidate for this university dance team. I was an adult (more or less) with experience in the working world—a grad student in the department of literature. Though not much older, the age gap felt like a chasm. Adulthood came with a healthy dose of social anxiety, an inability to take the plunge, head into a group of strangers to say, "hi." I opened my copy of *La Princesse de Clèves* and pretended the homework for my Novel Seminar was engrossing.

A young Indian girl, the team captain, waved her arms over her head to get our attention. Her thick black hair was pulled back into a ponytail. A thin film of black kohl outlined her large dark-brown eyes. I already knew her type: a sweet Indian girl who was using dance as a creative outlet while she pursued a practical major at the behest of her immigrant parents. Though I only had one desi parent, I had been witness to enough second-generation kids to know the family dynamic. In case you're losing count, that's one Indian immigrant parent (my father) and one non-Indian parent (my white/Midwestern mother). That equals one mixed daughter with serious identity issues and a lingering sense of inadequacy when it comes to 50 percent of her background.

Dancing had always interested me, ever since that one Saturday we visited my father's friends in Potomac, Maryland. I was ordered to play with the host's daughter. We were both six.

She led me to her room and knelt down next to a large box at the foot of her bed. "Wanna play with dolls?" She asked while fishing them out. She hadn't yet changed out of her dress from her Saturday morning Indian dance class—a light blue salwar kameez. The fabric had a sheen from the sunlight entering her bedroom window. I was entranced. She got to wear that *and* dance? Where could I sign up?

The dance I wanted to learn? Bhangra. One person beats a large double-headed drum, the dhol, while folks in colorful clothing move on the balls of their feet, twist their wrists, and stretch out their arms. It's an enchanting traditional dance; but somewhere in its migration from India to other countries, the dance snorted some cocaine and became frantic and hyper, choreographed to a conglomeration of Punjabi music and hip-hop. A way to get the general public more interested, I guess. Modern Bhangra was probably not what the farmers had in mind when they celebrated in villages long ago, but its origin made it my priority to master.

The Indian girl with the ponytail addressed our 40-odd group. I conjured her backstory, how her parents forced her to take cultural dance classes at an early age, how she wished to be more American, but would come home to a kitchen filled with strong aromas, a mother in a salwar kameez making roti over gas burners. She must have absorbed Hindi from her parents. She was most likely majoring in Political Science, because if she chose Dance, oh, the drama that would unfold! Her parents would stop paying her tuition. Probably disown her, too. While that would have made for a riveting soap opera, this girl knew how to walk that line, getting her adventures out *now* before she graduated and provided her parents with a litany of accomplishments to brag about. She assuaged her parents by informing them her current studies would lead to enrollment in a top-tier law school. In the meantime, she aced her classes and dated a white boy she'd NEVER tell her parents about.

The Indian girl explained to us that the team participated in competitions in the metro area and had taken home the first-place trophy for several years. The 20 available spots would go to the top candidates.

Competitions. Not my cup of chai. Too much pressure to be the best or disappoint your team and, by proxy, your family. Also, I wasn't here to compete. I just wanted to dance Bhangra because my Punjabi father hadn't cared to share anything related to his culture with me. He gave me an Indian name then returned to work as a surgeon and the primary breadwinner of the family. To him, assimilation was pragmatic. I was being raised in the United States, going to American schools. Why teach the girl to speak Punjabi when English was all she'd need? Echoes of my culture only wafted through the house when my father called India on the basement landline, yelling pleasantries on the phone with his sister and mother.

Most of the Indian décor and knickknacks were in our basement. I didn't know the meaning behind the statues of Shiva or our portraits of Guru Gobind Singh, but I wanted to. On Saturday afternoons, I descended into the basement to find my father on the rose sofa sectional watching *Mahabharata*, an epic story like *The Odyssey* only more desi. Produced in the late 80s the film spanned 30 VHS tapes. Actors in shiny gold and silver costumes spoke on the large screen. While it was of poor production value, the film harnessed my father's attention. It must have been comforting for him to get lost in a story in his native language, fully aware of the emotional cues and cultural guidelines. I tugged at my father's white undershirt and repeatedly asked, "What is he saying?" I wanted to be just as enraptured in the characters. I looked at his hooded eyes, his large cheeks with pock marks, his straight beak of a nose, and I hoped he'd let me in. But his eyes never moved from the television screen as he told me to go play outside.

* * *

In the auditions, I was assigned to "Group B." The actual studio spaces in the building must have been in use for the legitimate dance majors, because in order for us to get to work, an East Asian girl in jeans, a cotton shirt, and a jean jacket corralled me and 20 girls down the hallway of the lobby to a less-trafficked end of the building, near a floor-to-ceiling window.

The East Asian girl, our team "leader," lined us into three rows facing her, then walked us through the steps—just move our feet up and down like we were running in place. *Okay, I got this*, I thought. But then came the next combination, which required us to raise the right hand with the left leg and vice versa. My devotion to graduate school and internet memes did not prepare me for this amount of physical exertion. Within minutes, my heart was pumping faster than it had in months. My Oxford shirt stuck to the sweat on my back.

God, when was the last time I took a dance class? Was it back when I was a kid? After my father shooed me out of the basement, I petitioned my mother about Indian dance classes. Her face became blank. "I was not expecting this," she muttered as she had likely mentally scanned all the childrearing books she'd read and come up nil on "cultural heritage education." And there the issue of accessibility. Unlike my father's friends in Potomac, we didn't live in a dense South Asian community. Our small town of Upper Marlboro was the cultural mecca to a county courthouse and a Ledo Pizza.

My mother used her secret weapon: deflection. "How about ballet instead?" She asked. Waifs in pink tutus pirouetted through my mind. I nodded. Somewhere buried in the closet are photos of me in a pink leotard with black tights smiling shyly for the camera, my feet turned inwards in ballet slippers. I took classes in ballet, tap, and jazz. Unless Indians have a secret jazz dance I was unaware of, none was from my father's country.

As we practiced, the white girls to my right busted moves as if they had performed Bhangra since they were in diapers. *Oh God,* I thought. *I'm the slow kid!*

At the risk of making sweeping generalizations, I've found that Indian families—both in India and the ones that emigrated elsewhere—make education a priority for their children. My father, my grandfather, and my great-grandfather were no exception. I lived to please my family, so I proudly galloped home with top marks on quizzes and tests. The worst feeling was to sit in the classroom, feeling prepared and confident for an assessment while other students complained the material was too difficult. When immersed in a group whose opinions contradicted my own, my self-assuredness melted away. Panic would take over; I hadn't studied enough.

That feeling would return whenever I would get called out for not knowing enough about my Indian heritage. One arbiter was a guy from my neighborhood. Since we went to the same high school, he would sometimes drive me home. He and his hippie white family had lived in India for about a year when he was a boy. When he would reminisce about his childhood, he'd conjure those sentimental memories, wishing to return and munch on fresh mangoes. During one car ride, I admitted I didn't like the pulpy fibrous fruit. He chuckled, looked over at me from the driver's seat and said, "I'm more Indian than you!" The comment was so surprising, I couldn't articulate a response. He said it with conviction I could only guess came from never being questioned, yet I worried he might be right. A few years later, I moved into my freshman dorm room and met my roommate, a white girl from Virginia who had a love for Bollywood films. She spouted off her favorite desi actors like they were her cousins. I nodded like I knew of them. The truth: I had no idea. I unpacked my suitcases and propped my all-American DVDs in my appointed nook.

Our audition leader observed us, her mouth a straight line. Time to try the routine to music. She pressed play on the black stereo. A drumbeat started as she returned to her position at the front, her back to us. Then came our cue. I took a deep breath and let go, allowing my arms to stretch over my head, my legs to kick out at 90-degree angles. Muscles were in motion that I was sure had atrophied from inactivity. Finally, tension dissipated. I let the routine move through me. Without my inhibition, my body freely floated through the air, adrift in waves emitting from the speakers. I could see how Bhangra dancers made this effortless, how they were one with their movements, with the space around them.

There's often a difference between how you think you look and how you actually look. I was no Fred Astaire, or whatever the Indian equivalent would be. Shah Rukh Khan, perhaps? I made mistakes left and right. Or was it right and left? Bring up the arms and twist the wrists. Were my arms high enough? My moment of serenity bowed out and anxiety tagged itself into the ring. My shoulders tensed. My knees locked.

At the end of the song, the leader put her hands on her hips like Wonder Woman. Ten-minute break. A few girls trotted off together towards the bathroom.

During the break, I could make out my reflection clearly enough in the pitch-black window to rehearse the steps. My movements flowed, then stiffened. I kept second-guessing myself. With my hair tied back, I resembled my six-year-old self, a young girl trying to understand why people called me "the mixed kid" and why I never fit in. At home, my parents told me I was white, but outside, people kept asking me, "What are you?" White was never a satisfactory response. "You must be *something*," they'd press me.

As I practiced, part of me imagined how the Indian girl might take notice of my drive. My team leader would approach the Indian girl, guide her sightline to me, and murmur I wouldn't make the cut. But the Indian girl would put up her hand, motioning silence. "She's got spirit," she would say.

Before the tryout had begun, I'd contemplated pulling the Indian girl aside to tell her that I *was* in fact a fellow desi and see if that could be grounds for automatic entry. "Come on, I'm not like these white girls," I would say to her. Couldn't they just let me in? Bring displaced mixed girls back into the bosom of their heritage?

Then the actual Indian girl's voice boomed in the hall. The warm-up was officially over. The real auditions were about to begin. I sat on the floor with Group B as Group A lined up in front of a table where the Indian girl, our team leader, and the other judges sat.

With a click of the play button, the dhol beat started. Group A was off, a flurry of arms and legs. Unlike our group, the one performing included a handful of men with their own choreography. Together, it made for a complimentary coordination of graceful movements. How did they get these boisterous young puppies into formation, lined up like obedient soldiers, executing the moves like they were born to do it? Born to do it. Wasn't I born to do it? Right there before me, a team of white people completed choreographed moves after a mere thirty minutes of practice. A group with the same color of skin of people who had ostracized me my whole life outperformed me in an activity that was part of my heritage. At the time, I didn't have a strong grasp of how certain enterprises formed in the name of cultural exchange could still be exclusionary. These limber students didn't have bad intentions. They weren't aware they were a part of cultural theft, all in the name of winning. The Bhangra team, led by an Indian gatekeeper, had made a cultural dance a competition, where only the best (a.k.a., white) people participated. That all-too-familiar feeling returned: I wasn't Indian enough.

"Okay! Group B!" We took our places. The beat started.

I followed the routine to the best of my ability. Looking back, I wished someone had videotaped the audition. I felt I was following the moves as well as my partners were, but perhaps that sense of confidence was all in my head. Maybe, upon reviewing a replay, I would observe an older girl whose movements weren't precise or well-timed. An older girl who, instead, had performed an impressive impersonation of an orangutan. At any rate, we reached the end of the routine. My hands rested on my hips as I bent over for air.

The judges conferred again. Then the Indian girl said to expect a decision in a week.

During the quiet mornings in my studio apartment, barefoot in the middle of the hardwood floor, I danced for no one. Recalling the audition, I reenacted the practiced steps as sunlight peeked through the vertical blinds. During the week-long waiting period, I adopted Schrödinger's cat theory—basically, I was both on the team and not on the team. And if I potentially *was* on the team, it was high time to figure out how to bust a move without having to gasp for air. I hoped muscle-memory would solidify the steps. But then I'd hesitate, and my routine would end up a stilted, private performance.

I imagined calling my father and telling him I joined a Bhangra team. I tried to predict his reaction. Astonishment? Amazement? Indifference? I played out each possibility in my head and wondered if he'd recall those days his pesky daughter kept vying for his attention while he watched his movies.

Then the email arrived.

Due to the limited amount of space on our team for new members and the high volume of people interested in joining, we cannot offer you a position for this fall's AU Bhangra team.

I read the message a few times before the courteous rejection sunk in. Before I could crawl into the fetal position and soothe myself with coffee ice cream, I straightened up and formulated a response: *I'm not interested in competing, but do you think it would be possible if I could attend practice? You see, I'm Punjabi. I really want to learn the dance for myself and to learn more about my culture.*

My cursor wavered over the send button.

Why did I really want this? They were competitive entertainers. Not a cultural barometer for lessening my insecurity. The truth: it had never been about external validation. It was the pattern I couldn't break—descending those carpeted steps to the basement, the Hindi blaring from the television, my father reclining in peace. With acceptance into this dance troupe, I had gotten it into my mind that it would be enough to make my father turn, and finally see me.

With a click, I deleted the message. I picked up *Robinson Crusoe* where I had left it, with the pages faced down on the desk, a bird with outstretched wings.

This Side and That

by TONI ANN JOHNSON

from Aunt Chloe: A Journal of Artful Candor

When I pass on, my second son will arrive more than twenty minutes late to my funeral. With wild, dyed-dark hair in need of a cut and his Burberry overcoat rumpled, Philip will drag open the door to the stone chapel, causing it to creak and scuff against the slate-gray floor. He'll stand there stiff, wide-eyed, and bewildered as each head in every pew turns to stare at him, while my niece, May, reads the obituary that I'll have written myself.

Sighs and rolling eyes will shame him on my behalf as they add this offense to others: the time he went silent and shunned me for months, the many times he raised his voice, and the time he left me to die in a sub-par nursing home when he could have afforded better. But I'll receive this last act of aggression toward me without resistance or dismay because, in the end, I'll observe and accept, and I'll let things be.

Philip's un-shined shoes will flap up the aisle, Madeline's thin heels clicking behind him. My granddaughter, too, will be late because when I pass on she'll still be young enough to hope her father will do what he says. Get her to the church on time. Stop breaking the hearts of those who try to love him.

Lawrence, my first son, will glance at his lovely wife of thirty years and grit his teeth when his brother's foot loudly bumps the oak pew across from Velma, who'll frown at Phil, her ex, and tell herself she's there only to support her daughter and stepdaughter. This will be untrue. Velma will be there for herself. I'll understand. She once belonged and then she didn't, and exclusion was more than she could bear. I'll neglect to name her among those I've left behind because she won't be family when I go, but she will be there because she'll refuse not to be. Eventually, tenacity will win and she'll belong.

It'll be October. Cool and sunny rays will shine through the Tiffany stained glass windows. I might be resting in one of those rays, watching everything and hearing all.

Philip will slouch next to Madeline and behind his first daughter Livia, who'll have risen before dawn to drive to the Bronx from Boston with her baby and spouse, letting nothing, not her prestigious job nor her husband's, not infant car sickness or soiled and smelly diapers keep her from arriving on time.

Philip's stomach will growl though his morning tea with scotch and toast will have contributed to his lateness. He'll feel too warm in his suit. And he'll note with surprise all the people—so many—who'll be there to pay their respects. He'll think ahead to when it's his time and wonder: Who will show?

Family will be seated everywhere he looks, along with neighbors, friends, and members of my church, a community I'll have cultivated over six decades. He'll see, but not want to see, that though my way wasn't his way it didn't amount to less than his. When it's over, he'll see my little life had meaning.

He'll marvel at how I'll have stuck with those he fled because he wished for things the white world had like tennis clubs and homes with grounds and swimming pools, Swiss Alps ski-trips and women with slight buttocks. He believed those things were better.

When I pass on, Philip will tell himself his choice to leave one wife, and then another, was right for him. But a voice inside his head will ask *what if*? What if he'd stayed, put down roots, and watered them. What if he'd not destroyed two families? Would life have been worse had he nurtured the lives he made, or stuck with the community he came from?

The choir, dressed in blood red robes, will sing somber hymns I'll have chosen shortly before my demented mind slipped too far to reach.

With a ponderous face, Philip will sit, legs crossed, fingers stroking the hairs on his chin and he'll think that if his choices were mistakes he can trace them back to me. He'll remember the many times I pushed him away and days when my words were unkind. He'll believe I favored his brother. And sometimes I did. The music and voices that fill the church won't soften his ire or quell his clanging thoughts of my transgressions.

The melodies will, however, seep inside my granddaughters, and slip through fissures in armor they'll have cloaked around hearts, wounded by the ways their parents failed them, too. They'll tow resentments piled in childhood but, unlike their father, Livia and Madeline will long to let theirs go. When I pass on, they'll still be tender enough inside to hope they *can* release them.

I'll have done all I could to make things right with Philip. I will have offered apologies, written notes, letters, crocheted afghans, prayed, and made late night calls to say "I love you" before my earthly mind forgets the name and face I gave him and he puts me in a place where mothers of bitter sons wait to shed their shells and dance in the new dimension.

Before I lose my memory I will have learned that in mothering there is no making up for the love you fail to give. What you do, or don't do, with your offspring—the good and bad—makes the mold that shapes them.

Philip will work in a profession that talks endlessly about these molds. He'll lean back in his leather office chair, and chain smoke cigarettes while analyzing them, but the truth is, once set, they don't change. Still, he'll endeavor to mend the minds and hearts that yield from the shoddy molds (his own included) so they might shine in the world.

When I pass on I'll learn that, in the living, these defects, while sometimes ameliorated, are rarely fully healed or prayed away.

If this isn't the truth for all families, it will indeed be for ours. Wounds passed from my parents to me, and from me to mine will pass to theirs, and so on. And I'll watch from this realm, helplessly, as my progeny ticks forward in time with its pain. At first, I'll whisper to Livia and Madeline in dreams, *Don't be mad at your father* (their mothers aren't my fault), and they'll hear me, and yet not be able to let it all go.

After my burial, Phil will hug Livia and her baby goodbye, and after Madeline leaves for the subway with her cousin, he'll carry his wrinkled coat draped over the arm of his tailored suit, into the post-service repast where he'll linger longer than he planned to.

He'll ignore Velma across the room, chatting easily with my first son, Lawrence, and his family. He'll sit on a plastic folding chair and eat a second, then a third cucumber finger sandwich off a white paper plate. He'll make inconsequential conversation with old neighbors he deems unsophisticated because he'll have taken the day off and have nowhere better to go. And because, though he won't admit it, he'll miss me.

Long forgotten images will crack across his closed mind like lightning. He'll see me in my wide-brimmed blue hat smiling in the front row at his high school graduation. He'll recall the lemony scent of my 4711 cologne, and the smell of our kitchen when I made mint jelly from scratch. He'll feel me rubbing his tired, ten-year-old feet with witch hazel after he's walked home from school in the rain. He'll remember how I held his little hand in the hot Bermuda sun, when we skipped down the cobblestones past the tall steps of St. Peter's Church on the way to my mother's house.

He'll think I must be there somewhere among the simple people, sending these memories, and perhaps I will be, but the past will blaze in his thoughts because longtime friends and family from our old neighborhood—sweet smelling ladies wearing hat pins and carrying peppermints in their latch top purses—will regard him warmly and remind him of me; a me who's never done him wrong.

Philip will live alone at the time, in his tiny Greenwich Village flat, where his daughters will visit him infrequently and he'll serve them Jack Daniels coffee on a table stacked with matchbooks and mail. He'll boast of his numerous romantic conquests and at the same time he'll be seeing a thin white woman from his other world upstate. She'll be married, and soon she'll crush and discard him like a cigarette stub.

Not once will he visit my grave. He'll forget my birthday and speak ill of me. I won't hold it against him. He'll mistreat women continually. Sometimes he'll realize and more often he won't that, though I'll be long-gone, he'll never stop trying to get back at me for all I didn't give him.

Toward his own end, his girls will come to accept their father's flaws, though not condone them. When his mind goes, its decline will stir up past hurts. Neither daughter will abandon him. Nor will they take him in when he needs constant care. By then, he'll have a new sweetheart, pale and thin, like those before her. This one will be unmarried and live in the city, and she'll be kind. To the girls' astonishment she'll keep him, bedridden and babbling, in her Upper West Side high-rise until the day he's carried away.

One Monday morning in March, his love will leave for work and Philip will go into cardiac arrest with only an unlicensed home nurse from the Bronx by way of Jamaica to witness his soul's departure. She'll holler curses and prayers in patois and call 911 and the paramedics will restart his heart.

Though he'll have left his body to breathe via machine, he won't be ready to come when I call him. He'll think he still has things to do.

His girls will arrive by Tuesday morning. They'll sit with his brain-dead flesh and bones until Thursday evening when the tubes are removed.

That afternoon Velma will take the bus from Monroe, New York into Manhattan. Wearing gold earrings, bright lipstick, and heels, she'll be reading her local paper in the ICU waiting room as Livia and Madeline say goodbye. After the body expels its last breath, she'll join the girls, the girlfriend, and the home nurse from the Bronx, as they all walk east to have dinner in a skyscraper above Columbus Circle.

Velma will chat non-stop, enjoy the view and the high-end meal, and not notice Livia and Madeline's silence.

Despite having known their father's end was coming, its reality will stun them both. Fond memories of his presence at their graduations and weddings, and the many times he took them on adventures will light their minds in the days ahead, though not be bright enough to outshine the dark ones. They'll think of him with love, while still wishing he could have been better to them and their mothers.

When he finally gets where I am, he'll have had no homegoing at all, just a small gathering the girls arrange at a restaurant on Waverly Place. He'll have frequented its bar for years, sitting late into the night with his Dewar's on ice, writing an entire book about human mentality on yellow legal pads.

A few friends will attend, though only two from Monroe, his chosen, white, home away from home. Some of the small town connections will have passed on before him. Others will turn out to have not been true friends. I won't mention this when I see him.

Velma will insist on being in attendance, after first insisting on her inclusion in his obituary.

This I will comment on, and we'll share a good giggle.

A colleague will call the psychoanalytic theory he developed fascinating, audacious, and a work of genius. Family members from the Bronx and elsewhere will tell amusing stories of him rumbling with the boys in Mount Vernon, hitting on pretty girls with boyfriends, and climbing out his window onto the roof to stare at the stars. And while it won't be for me to understand, Philip will watch with glee and be profoundly pleased with his send off, miniscule though it may be.

When he arrives here, I'll be the second to embrace him, and smile into his eyes after his father, and he'll be amazed to find he's no longer angry with me. You can't be when you get here, because the scars made in life don't travel with you. Nothing hurts. And there's only love.

As far as what happened, and what's still happening on the other side, all you can do is observe, accept, and let things be. Together we'll wait for the rest of our beloveds and we'll look forward to nothing but goodness to share with them when they arrive.

Stalling: A Performance Piece

By JUANITA E. MANTZ

CHARACTERS

JUANITA, a Latina in her 40s stands at a podium in a dark theater with a spotlight on her. She is wearing a long, light blue dress. She has flowers in her hair. The piece begins in a comedic tone but then turns serious, then sad and ends on a poignant note.

JUANITA

I bought an electronic pregnancy test at Walmart. I was three days late and had to pee, so I ran into the bathroom with my cart, almost running over an elderly blue-haired lady on her walker.

I have never been good at waiting. One Christmas, many moons ago, my sisters and I discovered our Christmas presents in the attic and we opened them early and re-wrapped them. It spoiled Christmas that year for us kids, but my parents never found out until years later.

A picture of JUANITA and her two sisters at Christmas is projected onto a screen beside her. The picture is a Polaroid from the 1970s. The three young girls are wearing long nightgowns opening their presents smiling in front of a garishly decorated Christmas tree.

This would be the best present of all, I thought, as I entered that dirty bathroom stall with writing on the blue walls and torn toilet paper and seat covers on the floor.

JUANITA pauses. A picture of a dirty Walmart bathroom with blue stalls is projected onto the screen beside her.

But I did not care about the environment, it was an answer I was seeking. With teeth bared, I tore open the plastic wrap of the pregnancy test and pulled down my pants and underwear in one fell swoop and peed on the pink stick.

JUANITA places her hand on her chin and the light gets brighter and she shakes a bit as she speaks.

Pants pulled up, hand on my chin, I waited. I sat on the toilet and waited. I shivered with eagerness, aching for it. Maybe this was it. It was going to happen this time.

I would run home and scream over the phone to Adrian. "We did it, we made a baby!"

He would come home and cry and so would I and we would hold each other tight jumping in the air as one unit. A family.

JUANITA pauses and the Walmart picture is replaced with a picture of a pregnancy stick with a blank place where the answer would be and three dots like the stick is blinking.

The small symbol on the pink stick blinked and blinked. Maybe it was defective I thought.

I daydreamed of the cool clothes I would buy my kid. I would dress my child in black and white striped dresses, along with animal print and punk rock mini t-shirts. I would play "Asleep" by the Smiths and "Lullaby" by The Cure while I rocked the baby to sleep.

The lights dim back down as JUANITA rocks an imaginary baby in her arms while the song "Asleep" (instrumental excerpt) plays in the background while JUANITA sways along as if daydreaming, when the music ends she shakes herself awake.

Damn it, why was that stupid twelve dollar stick still blinking? Twelve dollars seemed like a lot, but I needed it to be a dependable answer. The day before, I had almost bought a test at the 99 Cent

Store. But I changed my mind knowing with certainty that 99 cents was way too cheap to be reliable.

The Walmart bathroom stall photo is projected on the screen beside JUANITA again.

As I peeked out the crack of the door frame to check on my shopping cart loaded with Diet Coke, soup and crackers, I started imagining Adrian, me and the baby in our house in San Bernardino.

I would cook for us. The baby would cry and I would smile, not minding it at all. Her cries were a sound I had been waiting for forever.

JUANITA's voice trails off and she pauses and says the next sentence in a dreamy tone.

Forever and ever...

JUANITA's voice turns more matter of fact and a picture of her in her USC Law school cap and gown is projected onto the screen beside her.

I waitressed my way through junior college after dropping out of high school five credits short of graduation to take my GED. Then transferred to undergrad. Finally, law school.

The next thing I know, I am at a big law firm with horrific hours. Then I waited for my husband Adrian to finish dental school. We thought we had all the time in the world, but we were wrong. It had taken mountains to be moved and miracles and thousands upon thousands of dollars in fertility treatments and the baby was going to be here, I could feel it.

JUANITA places her hand on her stomach and closes her eyes for a second.

A picture of her mom and dad with her and her two sisters is projected onto the screen beside her. Her voice rises hopefully.

And I would be the best mom. I would never yell or scream or throw things like my mom had. I would never come home drunk like my dad had.

JUANITA pauses and her voice turns deadly serious.

When I was little, I was deathly afraid of my mother. There was good mom and there was bad mom.

Good mom was like the mom on The Brady Bunch.

Nice mom bought us clothes, taught us to read, took us to our grandpa's house and reiterated the value of an education.

But bad mom was different.

My mom would come home from her waitressing shift, her eyes like big black buttons, her anger brought on by my dad not coming home.

When she screamed, "Get the Fuck Out!", we knew we had to run and fast. We would run to the park, a mere block away, and swing and swing. And I always wondered as a young girl, was everyone's life like this?

JUANITA's voice turns rueful and pragmatic.

But hey, I was over it. My parents did the best they could. I know that. Mom is different now. She never gets angry and Dad is up in the heavens. Yet, I couldn't help thinking, was this why I had waited so long. To be sure I was ready. To be positive I would not screw it up. Well, I was ready now. More than ready.

The Walmart bathroom stall picture is projected onto the screen beside JUANITA again and a toilet flushes in the background as JUANITA jumps up.

Someone flushed in the stall next to mine and I jumped up with a start.

A video of the pink stick is projected on the screen beside JUANITA and the stick is blinking.

The stick blinked one more time. I said a small prayer in my head.

There are no atheists in Walmart bathroom stalls.

Especially ones who are looking at a blinking pink stick, hoping for a positive affirmation of the possibility of finally creating a life at forty-three.

JUANITA clasps her hands in a prayer and looks up into the air as a picture of a blue sky with puffy clouds is projected onto the screen beside her replacing the pink stick.

"Look God, I know that I have asked for a lot, and you have given me so much," I whispered silently in my head. "But just give me this too."

A video of the blinking pink stick is projected on the screen beside JUANITA again.

The answer came as silent as my prayers and the word stood out sharply, in stark definition against the grey background of the pink digital stick.

The word NO appears on the screen beside JUANITA.

"No."

I threw the stick into the silver receptacle and I tried to shrug my sadness away.

JUANITA shrugs and grimaces and gives a raw rueful laugh.

Stupid stick. I hate Walmart.

The Walmart bathroom stall picture is projected onto the screen beside JUANITA again.

It was one thing to sit here and pee on the stick, but I was certainly above crying in a dirty Walmart bathroom stall.

Or was I?

No, I certainly was not.

JUANITA wipes a tear from her eye and leaves the stage.

CURTAIN

Coming Home, Midnight Blue

for Shahed, my forever homecoming date

by ARUNI WIJESINGHE

In the fall of 1985, a mutual friend sets us up. He encourages our first meeting, insists that we *look good together* and *would make a cute couple.* We are the two South Asians he knows; he says we should meet. We are not friends yet, but are aware of each other in the halls. As brown kids, we instinctively search for a pair of dark eyes, a nod of mutual acknowledgment. We enter October within the larger friend circle, slowly coming into one another's orbits.

Our mutual friend suggests we attend the homecoming dance together. This will be our first date, and my first date ever. Though I have had crushes in the past, I have never had to deal with the inconvenience of an actual boy. I am weeks away from turning sixteen and very green. I have zero experience. Ultimately, I am too shy and too curious to protest being paired with a relative stranger.

Three weeks before the dance my mom takes me to The May Company to buy a dress. The black satin skirt is voluminous with tulle crinoline and the lace bodice is the color of the dance's theme —"Midnight Blue"—a song I have never heard. On the way home from the mall, we stop at a fabric store to buy a spool of thread the same blue as my dress. It's something he can take shopping to buy a matching skinny tie. It is the first token I give a boy, a strand to tether us.

We spend Homecoming Week together, practice being a couple for Saturday night. He walks me to class, carries my backpack, sends me daffodils, delivered fourth period, the yellow bright against my trigonometry book. On that Friday we huddle on the bleachers at the football game, knees almost touching, and shiver against stadium benches in the cold October air. People smile at us, at our symmetry. We *make sense.*

We never question this artificial pairing. We *do* look right together. We are honor roll students and Spanish Club officers. We sit together on the quad during nutrition break and talk about college applications and the SATs. He walks me to class, helps me with my physics homework. Sometimes he drives me home from school in his tan pickup truck.

Neither of us is much into football, but we are part of the stadium crowd on Friday nights. We peg our jeans, wear high-top Reeboks. We listen to Tears for Fears, flip through the stacks of LPs at Tower Records with our friends. We exchange valentines, taping red envelopes to locker doors. We never bring leftovers to school, always opt for sack lunches of turkey sandwiches or share fries from the school snack bar. I understand Sinhala and he Urdu, but we never mention these superpowers at school. Instead, we practice our verb conjugations and plan potlucks for Spanish Club. Though neither of us celebrates Christmas at home, we exchange gifts like other couples at school. These are the rites we perform to assert our American-ness. It is the toll we pay as children of immigrants. We think we are transforming into typical American teenagers; we never once realize the folly of trying to become what we already are.

We don't push against the walls of the boxes in which we are placed. Instead, we embrace our shared brownness, find fraternity in fingertips that smell of cardamom and coriander. And though expectation pairs us, we see ourselves in one another. The recognition is both astonishing and reassuring. We make no excuses to one another for strict curfews or test prep weekends. No need to explain fathers who answer the door wearing hand-loomed cotton sarongs. He understands the new year puja and I don't question his Ramadan fasts. We never fear the rejection of parents who balk at our names, who will mispronounce us for the rest of the school year. We fit easily into the same reality of rice and curry, prayers in languages neither of us speak, the pressure to achieve in a world that would hold us back.

We are not on the ballot for Homecoming King and Queen of 1985. We don't need rhinestone crowns to feel dominion over our high school lives. We have the smell of carnations, his dad's gold Ford Thunderbird, and a tweed tie that matches the lace on my dress. We leave the dance, our fingers interlaced. We walk to the school parking lot, into the blue midnight.

My Wife Who Became My Husband

by CARLA R. SAMETH

from Metroweekly D.C.

He has begun to sound more mannish,
as if we were in an old-time movie,
maybe "My Fair Lady"— he's as grumpy as Professor Higgins.
I'm not saying he wasn't a curmudgeon before
but the first days after his top surgery, it was as if
he'd awoken in his real body—
this new "he" and "my Husband"—
and I was moved by his happiness
as if he'd finally landed on the right planet. But then,
I suppose the anesthesia and pain pills wore off
and there was a downward movement
as if the plane went into a tailspin.
He says he has no regrets but perhaps some
resentment that he couldn't have been born
into the right body the first time around. After
that I couldn't seem to locate the euphoria,
the sweetness of those early post-surgery days
when I could tend to him, and even with his pain
he looked upon it all with wonderment,
as if he'd tunneled out the birth canal again, the right gender.

This is not what I had in mind when I married
that woman,
the leap into removing those lovely breasts
that were so sexy with the other masculine
trappings, her manera de ser. Butchy but tender.

six-pack fit and tough, yet vulnerable,
hair tied back, neatly pinned to the top,
military style. The first time I saw her
after we'd met, she was waiting for me, leaning
against a building at California Plaza,
La Santa Cecilia playing in the background.

We've both gained weight since we married in 2016.
Rocky Road and streaming television are sometimes
what holds us together. He's got angry scars
on his chest and the tone of his voice often matches
with raw irritation. I am always asking too much
because he's working full-time, in school full-time,
taking two courses at another university.
And getting shots of testosterone.
But I'm a long-hauler.

My third marriage, I no longer resort
to fight-or-flight as the only options.
I remember the photo the documentary photographer
took of "still-her" the night before surgery,
the light was just so, duskish, and
she lay back, arm behind her head,
shirt off, those sexy blue shorts that matched our
Mexican-blue bedroom wall, her blue blue eyes.
A badass look, breasts falling just so and still there.
Tough, languid even, but sensual.

It has been almost a year now.
Let me just say that he is happy
with this new adolescence,
this coming of age. When puberty
first hit him as a girl he offered to give
the breasts away to those who complained of having none.

He gleefully shaves the facial hair
that begins to crop up. His acne, a welcome
sign that change is happening.
I see the He appearing every day.
begin to see that mixture of shadow
and light again.

This is who I always was he tells me
as he emerges from the chrysalis.
He says he wants to be
"the right kind of man." Think tender.
Think learning to listen, to not
run from the feelings. Think
social justice fighter. Nonviolent.
My longing for something
different, a woman, is eclipsed by
my love for this person that dared
to make this change at 45. To be the man
he always believed he was.

Discord

by KELLY BOWEN

On the third night of a 2021 camping trip with my daughter, my world fissured.

Camping had become our thing in the early months of COVID. Our necessary reprieve from the world, the magic of nature also wove through Aidyn causing her to break open and share with me what she'd feared sharing.

The previous summer, she came out to me. I knew Aidyn wasn't straight. After all, she's *my* daughter... and she's so like me.

But I was not prepared for what she revealed this time.

Like many teens these days, she has a robust personal world... online. COVID required it, and her natural predilection for technology and the ease of hiding behind the screen honed it in.

I had just cracked open a canned cocktail after a lovely day of hiking. The plan was to sit for a bit before dinner and a campfire.

I handed her a small glass of what I was drinking because I'm *that* mom.

She played some stupid game on her phone. I journaled, hiding my annoyance that even without us having cell service, she was on tech.

The six miles seeped into me. The calm of the trees and the crisp mountain air lulled me. Or maybe it was the alcohol.

My reverie was broken by the sound of my daughter bursting into tears. I looked up in alarm.

She gasped, "Mom. I'm so worried about Aki. She keeps telling me she's going to kill herself. I can't talk to her! What if she *does* something?"

Aki was one of her online friends, a twenty-one-year-old girl who lived with her parents in England. She was mute, so it made sense that the internet was her world. And it made odd sense that she had grown so close to my fifteen-year-old open-minded, big-hearted daughter.

But I didn't like Aki. Aki was super dark. My daughter was already battling depression. That Aidyn had suicidal ideations and had been cutting had been a revelation earlier in the year, after she fainted in front of me, and I ended up taking her to Rady Children's Urgent Care. She was in intensive therapy and psychiatric care. I was trying desperately to keep her from the dark side. My instincts screamed about Aki. But what could I do without alienating Aidyn? And where was the risk when this too old other kid was in England?

Panic flooded me at the magnitude of her anxiety attack. Stamping it down, I turned to her. "Honey, that's terrifying for sure, but love, if you could text her, what would you be able to do?"

"I don't knooooowww," she sobbed as I held her.

When she regained the ability to speak, she said, "Mom. I have to tell you something."

I suddenly wished I hadn't had a cocktail.

"Aki ... is ... my girlfriend. We're in love. She's my *soulmate.*"

I felt the ground shift under me. My kid is precocious, but what twenty-one-year-old wants to be with a fifteen-year-old who's across the planet? The illogic of it all hit me. But I immediately recalled my teenage years. When I was fifteen, my mom didn't like my best friend. She pronounced her a bad influence and decreed I was never to see her again. I dug my heels in and held onto that friendship with the ferocity of a terrier with a rat in its mouth. My mom turned out to be right, but the way she handled it was so wrong, I ended up far more damaged by that friendship than if she'd let me figure it out.

I wasn't going to repeat my mom's shitty parenting. I needed to know more, without pushing Aidyn away.

I tried to sound interested as well as properly concerned.

"So, what's your plan? Still going to college?" I bit down on the bile that formed thinking what if she isn't.

"I am."

"Oh good. Are you... thinking... England or here?"

"As soon as I graduate from high school, Aki is coming here."

I nodded. At least she wasn't planning on running to England.

"Does Aki being mute... bother you at all? I mean her ability to communicate with you will be limited, and kid... you're kind of verbal. How will it feel to never hear the words "I love you"?"

She shrugged, though I could see wisps of thought cross her mind.

"I'll be fine. I'll learn sign."

I paused. I was about to walk on the edge of a sinkhole.

"You know, honey, there's a lot of age difference between you two."

"*Mom*, when I'm thirty and she's thirty-six it won't matter."

I couldn't believe she threw *that* line at me.

I almost rolled my eyes.

But there was a bigger worry digging at me, though I didn't have the pulse of it yet. And I needed her to understand that Aki wasn't good for her without my decreeing she had to end it.

"Well, honey, I'm happy for you," I forced out around my teeth. Looking for an inroad I carefully tossed out, "I do need to say though, the age thing... Aki is an adult, and you're a minor. There *are* statutory rape laws..."

She blanched slightly, before digging in her heels.

"Oh, that's why Aki isn't coming until I'm eighteen." She nodded. Problem solved.

The next month saw me trying to worm out what was bothering me, beyond Aki being too old and seemingly content to live in her parents' home doing nothing for her future. Beyond stirring the depression in my kid.

I spoke to my therapist about a cut on Aidyn's arm which I was sure she lied about and how I was worried she was still suicidal.

"You have to read her messages," my therapist said.

I dropped my jaw. I hated that idea. Aidyn having privacy was a fundamental moral code of mine. To read her private communications was forbidden.

"It's not about violating her privacy," my therapist continued, without me saying a word. "It's about keeping her safe."

I let the words fall over me. It wasn't crawling through her things for information I didn't need to know. Suicidal ideation far outweighed privacy. "Ok," I stammered, feeling queasy, "You're right."

But how was my next problem. I was working from home, but Aidyn was home too. How could I look when she was always around?

Two days later, an unexpected opportunity presented itself.

"I'm going to the garage to do some art," she pronounced, heading outside.

I got up from my desk for more water and walked past her now empty bedroom. She'd left her pc on. The Discord app chat window was still open.

Looking around like a kid about to get caught rifling through her parent's bedside table drawers, I dashed into her room and sat on the chair. I scrolled madly, while keeping an ear for footsteps. Breaking her lies about cutting was critical, but I could *not* let her catch me.

I found clear evidence of the level of Aidyn's obsession with Aki, and the fragility of the situation. Aki regularly talked about suicide, and Aidyn was terrified. Aki was Aidyn's world. And me? They decried me a nosy, clueless adult. Aki promised to help Aidyn be free of me. I would never interfere with them. Their love was too great.

I *didn't* find anything about cutting. But I was chewing on something bigger, something that hadn't yet made itself clear to me.

I could feel the risk of being caught increasing even as I wanted to scream.

I scrolled to the latest message, hoping to God I hadn't made it look like I'd been in the thread.

Over the next week, I seized every opportunity to tap her messages. The best was a two-hour long driver training session. But stupid me? I didn't have her passwords.

Before the session, she had a pc problem. She asked for my help. I stood over her as she logged in, and watched her hands type her password, determined to catch every key stroke, somehow managing despite her speed on the keys.

One wee win.

The instructor showed up. As soon as the car pulled away, I ran into her room.

Naively, I was still looking for cutting revelations. I was desperate to be right. I scrolled fiercely to reach messages from where she'd cut while we were camping and lied about it.

Instead, the bottom of my cracked world crumbled under me.

Aidyn was sending Aki nude photos, though the photos themselves had been deleted from the thread. She was calling Aki "mommy" and her dom. She was watching BDSM videos. My kid who'd not even had a first kiss yet! There was a sick depravity to it. Clear evidence of my child ... my *child!* ... being manipulated by an adult.

I wanted to puke.

I snapped some screenshots. But in my hysteria, I still fixated on proving the tamer issue of cutting.

Time ran out. I returned her machine to how it had been when she left.

I was beside myself, queasy from the sexual things I'd read. Not in a prudish way of a mom denying her daughter is a human. But what I saw was distorted, and violent. And it was with a sick fuck of an adult.

This was bigger than me. I needed help. I shared it all with a trusted friend. She responded unexpectedly. She told me to lean in. Suggested I tell Aidyn I was booking a trip for us to England.

I bucked so hard. I wasn't going to make a fucking trip to England!

My friend clarified. She wasn't saying we'd *actually* go. But saying we'd go would let me see what reactions would come.

Her words landed. So ... I leaned in, letting the idea percolate in my subconscious.

A few days later, I took Aidyn to dinner. I asked her to leave her phone at home. At dinner, I acted interested, as if I embraced this partnership.

And then I asked Aidyn to schedule a zoom with her, Aki, and me.

Aidyn paled.

I insisted.

She demanded I set it up.

I told her no: her person, her task.

The ride home was quiet.

Aidyn set up a Discord text chat with her, me, and Aki, yelling through the house, "There, now you can get to know Aki."

I played along. A little.

The next day, coming home from an event, I asked if she'd set up the zoom. "No! Aki isn't comfortable on video. Can't you just use text?"

"Naw, I want to zoom honey. Don't you want your person to know me as much as me them?"

"Then *you* set it up!"

She sounded like a five-year-old, not someone ready for life partnership at the whopping age of fifteen.

"No. Your job sweetie."

She fell quiet.

When we got home, she slammed her door. I could hear fierce typing.

Fifteen minutes later, she emerged angry. "Mom! Aki isn't comfortable! Can't you just *text* her?"

I repeated my need for a zoom.

Then Aki texted. "I understand you want a zoom," she sent. "But even before COVID, I was never comfortable being seen. I walk around with a hoodie over my head."

I said I wouldn't judge how she looked.

Aki dug in her heels. She didn't understand why it had to be my way. Texting was all I needed.

Which is when I got mad.

I fired off, "*I* don't understand why you think it's appropriate to tell the mother of your *girlfriend* how it will or won't be. Everyone else I know looks to *impress* the parents of their significant other."

Aki demanded, "Am I not allowed an opinion on how things are done?"

"No," I typed. "My daughter is a *minor*."

Aki sent, "I've not committed one thing to your daughter that might make me a predator."

I stood up straighter. I had suspected she ... or he ... was a predator, but *I* hadn't said those words. "I'm asking for one zoom."

"I decline."

"You *decline*?"

"A zoom isn't necessary to get to know me."

"It is for me."

Aki stopped texting.

A moment later, Aidyn emerged from her room in hysterics. Aki had just said they were done, that it was for the best, and then had gone quiet.

I had installed a program a week prior on my internet router, which allowed me to control access by device. As Aidyn came to me, enraged and terrified of losing Aki, I hit a button in the application for the program on my phone. When she saw me click her photo in the app, she freaked out more.

"What did you do? What did you *do*?"

"I shut off your access to the internet so we can talk."

She lost any remaining control.

I let her rage. Let her cry.

She insisted on how wrong I was. She was devastated to have lost Aki.

I kept repeating, "All I asked for was a zoom, honey. Don't you want your person to want to know me?"

Things started to click for her, but she was still crying and raging.

Aidyn's disbelief and fear made me aware of a layer of my own unwillingness to fully accept what had been transpiring. Deep inside, part of me had believed the zoom would happen, and that in order to set it up, I would get Aki's email address from which I would be able to search the internet for real information about her. I had held onto the idea that Aki loved my daughter, if in some distorted and sick way. In that moment, I came face to face with what was so terrifying as to be unthinkable.

I cracked. I released my biggest fear. "Honey," I said, pulling up a webpage. "Discord is on the 2021 dirty dozen list of sites for internet predators." I showed her the headline. Then I scrolled down. "And honey... you're on the last step. I'm terrified someone is going to show up at the house, steal you, and sex traffic you."

Her face reflected shock. She read the stages of grooming. I watched as she put it all together.

Her anger turned to horror as she admitted she had never seen this person on video. That the photos she'd gotten could have been of anyone.

She crumpled into my arms.

We spent the rest of the night with her crying. But it was only a few minutes after she'd realized I was right that she also started raging against what had been done to her.

Somehow, not only had I managed to navigate this horror without pushing her away, I had drawn her closer.

In the following days, I filed a claim with the FBI. They took Aidyn's phone. But in the time between my first diving in and the culmination, Aki had deleted key texts from the thread. The agent said it was glaringly clear what had been going on, but there wasn't enough legal evidence for a case. They copied Aidyn's phone so that if there was another case, perhaps it would help them break it.

He could see I was upset. He explained. In the battle for resources, I was an involved parent of an older kid, and I'd gotten her out.

My being a *good* parent meant I would have to live with my unquenchable desire to find and end that asshole. There would be no resolution for me or Aidyn.

The agent handed me Aidyn's phone but told me he shouldn't give it back. The nude stills and videos of her in her camera roll made *me* guilty of possessing lewd photos of a minor. Go home, he said, and wipe her phone.

As if returning my property was a big thing he could do for us...

Aidyn is doing better these days. Her meds are working. She even had a real girlfriend last year, replete with the innocence of the first time holding someone's hand.

And we're closer than ever. To keep it that way, I'll make sure we camp, every year.

I've never lost my belief in the importance of Aidyn having privacy. So, when I wrote this story that is both mine *and* hers, I asked if she was ok with it. I asked if she was ok with my sharing it. I told her if she changed her mind, I would withdraw.

But each time I ask, she gives me consent.

Because my kid? She doesn't want this to happen to anyone else.

Yes, I Am

by ELLINE LIPKIN

that woman wandering the grocery store,
unkempt, bedraggled, and babbling
more than the baby, trailing Cheerios
through the legholes saddled inside the cart.

Moving towards each another, we daven,
head bent to catch each syllable-wisp,
murmuration set inside the messy tendrils
earth-esque waft which lingers from where you were before.

Once pitted at my center, now our umbilicus
is elsewhere, yet my body is still where you latch.
This, too, will fall away, with your starfish eyelashes,
and thick-coated baby voice, sheened with wonder.

But now, a white spark, my blue star,
we draw in, both know nothing but this flailing
yearning, the settling of heat, the urge to cocoon,
naked to every hour, barely functional in public.

Poem in Which the Subject Does Not Appear

for my siblings

by ELLINE LIPKIN

Empty years   stain   a silence

once white ned   with unknowing   our triumvarate

in even spaces   gaps   instead

secret   too easy   billows

the   ransacked   future.

a trio set   now leached   to seeded dregs

each   draught   the taste

of ruin

The Disfellowshipped

Based on true life events

by THEA PUESCHEL

CHARACTERS

MATURE BAARA, 46
BROTHER THOMAS, 70
CHORUS OF BROTHERS
YOUNG BAARA, 21

SCENE I-1: DARKNESS

The present, Darkened theater, Evening

PLACE

A theater with the house LIGHTS OFF, a LOUD FAN turns on, filling the space with WHITE NOISE and cool air.

MATURE BAARA *(Offstage in a hushed tone)*

If I let go of hiding, I can make room to be seen.
If I let go of silence, I can make room for my voice.
If I let go of protecting, I can make room to protect myself.
If I open my heart, I can make room for joy.
If I let go of being shunned, I can make room for community.
If I let go of perception, I can make room for reaction.
If I let go of toxicity, I can make room for hope.
If I let go of my tongue, I can make room for words.
If I let go of bargaining, I can make room for acceptance.

SCENE I-2: BAARA CONFRONTS HER MOTHER

Empty Stage, Night

An empty rocking chair sits center stage. Lights RISE on the rocking chair.

MATURE BAARA walks in and sits in the rocking chair. She rocks forward and leans toward the audience.

MATURE BAARA

I remember when we were little, Bela and me. You would tell us about how you hid when the Witnesses came.

MATURE BAARA knocks on the arm of the rocking chair.

When you and dad were first married, back then you were just a girl yourself.

She rocks forward and gets out of the chair and walks behind it.

One day, they knocked, and they saw you through the window.

She hides behind the chair and peeks out.

You thought about jumping behind the couch, but you realized how silly that would be. They had already seen you. So, you answered the door.

BEAT

...and you would finish with, and that, girls, is how we became Jehovah's Witnesses.

MATURE BAARA laughs and shakes her head.

They were so nice, so welcoming, so unconditional.

BEAT

You couldn't resist. They offered the family support you never had.

BEAT

You felt fully loved for the first time.

She walks around to the front of the rocking chair and sits down. That's how we became Witnesses. It was your hunger for storge, philia and agape.

She knocks on the armrest of the rocking chair.

You know, I never got it. The whole not being able to hide thing.

A phone RINGS.

Until my phone rang twenty-five years ago.

BEAT

Five years before that, I remember my panic and fear. You had started to disappear. Your tears and depression were never ending, and I wanted to make it all go away. I knew Jehovah was <u>your</u> only hope. So, I planned to get baptized. When I told you, the face that I used to recognize beamed with pride. You forgot you were broken for a minute. What I didn't tell you—

BEAT

"The truth,"

MATURE BAARA puts her fingers in quotation marks.

Has always rested dead in my heart.

BEAT

Since my first time on stage at the Kingdom Hall, I must have been three or four and that tall Brother asked me if I wanted to go to paradise, and I said no. He laughed. The congregation laughed. But I knew even back then, in that moment, I didn't want to go, and I didn't believe. I wasn't about to pet lions and zebras in perfect harmony, no matter how he rephrased the question or hard the congregation laughed.

She shrugs.

When I was sixteen, I thought I could save you—from the stress stroke, from your broken heart, from the other pain. I thought I could be your salvation. But you couldn't even see me.

BEAT

That's why I quickly jumped in that above ground pool in my polka-dotted bathing suit at the Circuit Assembly and let two Brothers in white t-shirts and board shorts drown me of my senses.

All that, to see if I could reappear to you. Immediately after my eyes burned with chlorine, when I opened them, I saw the distortion and the flaw of my actions.

MATURE BAARA bites her lip.

Do you remember a few months before my baptism, my friend Patrick killed himself? In the boy's bathroom in the 200 block of the high school? I couldn't go to the funeral because it was at the Catholic church.

BEAT

That was Junior year, it was fucked; I mean fluffed. It messed me up. I couldn't use public bathrooms for three years. Did you know that?

She shakes her head.

A few weeks before I held my breath and was submerged, we were visiting Grandma and you told me to watch *Dead Poets Society*. You swore it was a good movie, that it would make me feel better.

She rocks forward and laughs.

Having your kid watch a movie about a kid who killed himself, after their friend killed themselves? Well, that was kind of epic.

She taps her fingers on the armrest and scrunches her face.

You said you didn't remember the suicide part of the film. It was pivotal. How could you forget?

OFFSTAGE a phone RINGS, an answering machine BEEPS, and MATURE BAARA looks offstage.

BROTHER THOMAS (offstage)
Hello Baara, this is Brother Thomas. We'd like to talk to you.

MATURE BAARA
Twenty-five years ago, I couldn't hide.

MATURE BAARA fights to hold tears back.

You gave them my number.

SCENE I-3: YOUNG BAARA MEETS WITH THE BROTHERS

Meeting room, Kingdom Hall, Day

A folding chair in the middle of the stage is surrounded by three other chairs in a halfmoon shape. YOUNG BAARA sits CENTER STAGE wearing a modest dress. The other chairs remain empty and in darkness. She sits down. TAPE HISS fills the background.

YOUNG BAARA
I had a choice. I could live a lie, or I could live in my truth and hurt you. As you know, I chose the latter.

BROTHER THOMAS *(offstage)*
Do you know why you are here?

YOUNG BAARA

(Looks at the audience)

I could think of a thousand ways that I had sinned, but I wasn't going to tell them. It wasn't their business.

CHORUS OF BROTHERS *(offstage)*

There have been reports of you engaging in inappropriate behavior.

YOUNG BAARA fidgets in her chair and adjusts her modest dress to cover her knees.

BROTHER THOMAS *(offstage)*

You've been smoking.

CHORUS OF BROTHERS *(offstage)*

Have you ever engaged in heavy petting?

YOUNG BAARA

(Looks at the audience)

It always seemed that the sisters were disfellowshipped more often than brothers in the congregation. I remember you telling me that was because they couldn't hide their sin.

YOUNG BAARA pantomimes a pregnant belly.

A poor girl would be sitting at the back of the Kingdom Hall being ignored by everyone.

BEAT

Publicly shunned. A few months later with baby in tow and back in the good graces of the Elders, that same girl that spent six months or more ignored would be love bombed by every brother and sister in the room once reinstated.

BEAT

But my circumstances were different. There wasn't any evidence. Just reports.

BROTHER THOMAS *(offstage)*

Is there anything else you would like to tell us?

CHORUS OF BROTHERS (offstage)

You don't have to quit smoking. You just have to repent.

YOUNG BAARA shakes her head.

CHORUS OF BROTHERS (offstage)

Go to meetings. Follow the rules, and you'll be fine.

YOUNG BAARA

(Looks at the center chair and takes a deep breath)

No.

The CHORUS OF BROTHERS and BROTHER THOMAS GASP.

YOUNG BAARA (cont'd)

My parents raised me too well to be a hypocrite. I won't sit down with you and your brothers and sisters and have you cast judgment upon me for doing something that is harmful, but not morally wrong. I won't.

The LIGHTS TURN OFF abruptly.

SCENE I-4: THE BROTHERS ISSUE THEIR JUDGMENT

The past, Darkened theater, Evening

House lights off, a LOUD FAN turns on, filling the space with WHITE NOISE and cool air. Several microphones CRACKLE.

CHORUS OF BROTHERS *(offstage)*

It is with great sadness that we announce Baara Fournier has been disfellowshipped and is no longer a Jehovah's Witness. We encourage you to uphold the scriptural arrangements of disfellowshipping and follow the guidelines to avoid temptation.

Microphone INTERFERENCE, the SPOTLIGHT focuses on YOUNG BAARA. The rest of the stage remains in darkness.

YOUNG BAARA

I knew what was coming, thanks to 1 Corinthians 5:11. A biblical decree to not associate with a fallen person such as myself.

Microphone INTERFERENCE, the SPOTLIGHT DIMS on YOUNG BAARA.

CHORUS OF BROTHERS *(offstage)*

It is with great sadness that we announce Baara Fournier has been disfellowshipped and is no longer a Jehovah's Witness. We encourage you to uphold the scriptural arrangements of disfellowshipping and follow the guidelines to avoid temptation.

Microphone INTERFERENCE, the SPOTLIGHT focuses on YOUNG BAARA. The rest of the stage remains in darkness.

YOUNG BAARA

2 John 9:11 would ban me from greetings and being received in homes.

Microphone INTERFERENCE, the SPOTLIGHT DIMS on YOUNG BAARA.

CHORUS OF BROTHERS *(offstage)*

It is with great sadness that we announce Baara Fournier has been disfellowshipped and is no longer a Jehovah's Witness. We encourage you to uphold the scriptural arrangements of disfellowshipping and follow the guidelines to avoid temptation.

Microphone INTERFERENCE, the SPOTLIGHT focuses on YOUNG BAARA. The rest of the stage remains in darkness.

YOUNG BAARA

I was an unrepentant—

BEAT

A wrong doer. 1 Corinthians 5:6,7 was a call to action to protect the congregation from corruption. My name and the warnings were announced three times, or so I was told.

BEAT

And just like that.

YOUNG BAARA

SNAP, the lights go OUT.

I was alone. No family. No friends. No community.

SCENE I-5: YOUNG BAARA MEETS HER FUTURE SELF

The past/present, Darkened theater, Evening

House lights off, a LOUD FAN turns on, filling the space with WHITE NOISE and cool air. The lights come up. YOUNG BAARA stands behind a rocking chair. MATURE BAARA sits in the chair.

YOUNG BAARA

If I live my truth, I can be free.

If I release betrayal, I can find trust.

If I trust my core, I can make room for my future self.

If I do not waiver, I can find myself.

If I do this, I do it for future me.

YOUNG BAARA walks off stage. The SPOTLIGHT is on MATURE BAARA. The light gets BRIGHTER.

CURTAIN

Flare-Up

by NORIKO NAKADA

When I'm eight, I notice Mom hasn't been feeling well. She's sore and tired, so she goes to the doctor. They tell her she has rheumatoid arthritis and give her pills to help with the pain and swelling. Sometimes Mom's fingers puff up so big she can't wear her wedding ring. Sometimes, I have to sit in the front seat of the car because she can't shift the car into reverse without my help.

I try to figure out what causes Mom's flare-ups, when she rubs her hands together like she's washing them because the joints hurt, and she moans as she gets up from the couch. Sometimes the flare-ups come when it rains, and I wonder if Mom is dying because she stays in bed all day. On other days, when it's sunny and the sky is a perfect blue, Mom struggles gripping her toothbrush.

Then, like magic, she feels better. She starts a new medication and it works. She smiles again, and has energy to take us to school, the park, the grocery store.

On hot summer days, Mom likes to take afternoon drives with the air conditioning on high. There was a forest fire south of town last week, so Mom drives us to see it. We listen to the radio and head down highway 97. We turn onto a small dirt road and the radio fades to static. My brother and I sit in the back seat, looking out the windows at the towering pine trees.

In a flash, the forest turns from green to black. Mom drives slowly on the soft dirt road where there are no trees, no chipmunks, no sagebrush. There is nothing alive at all. We are the only car on the road, driving where the fire just burned and smoke still drifts up from the ground where trees used to grow. The car starts to smell like fire and Mom turns the air conditioning down. We don't talk and just stare at a world that looks like the inside of a wood stove.

"How did it start?" I ask, mesmerized by the destruction.

Mom isn't sure.

"Are you sure they put it all out?" I imagine our car surrounded by an unexpected flare-up just like when Mom can hardly get out of bed and it hurts for her to stir oatmeal or flip pancakes.

"Yes, Honey, I'm sure they put it out," Mom says with a certainty she never has when she talks about her arthritis. Mom turns the car around slowly. She puts the car in reverse, and I watch her shift from reverse to first, reverse to first, fearing the next flare-up.

How to Tell Her

by SANDY YANG

from Flyway

The last three months were the worst of Alice's life. It started when her ex-husband died after a long battle with cancer. They had not spoken to each other since the split, not even when he got sick. Alice only went to the funeral to comfort their daughter, but Kaylee wouldn't even look at her, as she stood at the door of the church, greeting the mourners one by one. It depressed Alice to see her daughter's hair cut so short, making the shapeless gray dress she was wearing look like a centuries-ago men's nightgown.

Shortly afterward and without notice, Alice came home from a weekend getaway with her boyfriend, Ian, to find her roommate had vacated their apartment. When Alice asked Ian to come live with her, he said yes but delayed the move for two months, before admitting he was still married. Not only had she lost her boyfriend, but Alice had to find a new roommate fast or she'd lose her rent-controlled apartment in Santa Monica. So far, all the people she interviewed were a bit off. One was hypersensitive to sound, even to a bird chirping outside the window. Another inquired about the toxic chemicals in her furniture, and asked if she would be open to getting rid of all her furniture. The last one even insulted Alice for being Chinese and blamed her for the plight of the Tibetans. No wonder these people were looking for roommates at their age! By now, everyone normal and Alice's age had formed a family, learned to settle down and be content. The thought that Alice was one of those other people who had no family and no contentment was so depressing, she cried every night to sleep.

All the while, Alice had meant to call her daughter and ask how she was doing. She even thought of driving up to the Valley, where Kaylee had returned to college, but Alice kept putting it off until she could put it off no longer. Her baby was going to turn twenty-one, and it would be her first birthday without her father. To prepare for the call, Alice applied a matte foundation so her face wouldn't appear shiny on FaceTime, and then she found a spot in the kitchen where the foggy autumn light might help the filters soften her features even more. Finally, she took a deep breath and looked for her daughter's number in her contacts list. As expected, Alice's call went to voicemail. Kaylee didn't even record a personal greeting, but opted for the robotic voice to enunciate each numeral of her phone number.

After the beep, Alice sang "Happy Birthday," and then got nervous and rambled about taking her out today, but if her friends were taking her out (and of course they were), then next week or anytime would also be great, if she could spare a few hours to see her mother. Finally, Alice said she loved her and missed her.

A minute after she ended the call, Alice received a text from Kaylee: *buying a mattress today. We can have lunch nearby if you want*

Alice wondered why she needed to buy a mattress. Didn't she live in a dorm? Didn't the college provide beds and mattresses? She wouldn't ask via text, and only replied: *YES*

Kaylee sent a link to a taco place in the Valley, located in a strip mall next to a mattress store.

Alice texted: *Let me take you somewhere nicer. How about Santa Monica, Venice, DTLA*

Kaylee did not reply, so Alice started researching trendy restaurants on her phone and sent links to three possible candidates. Kaylee wrote back: *buying a mattress at noon today*

***

It was on the drive to the Valley that Alice had first thought of asking Kaylee to move in with her. Even she dismissed the idea at first, believing her daughter would never go for it, but if her dorm neglected to provide a mattress, then maybe she would be open to leaving. Rent wasn't an issue either, since Kaylee would have inherited all of her father's retirement and savings accounts. And besides, it was about time they reconnected after her father had turned their only child against Alice. He may have looked the part of a good father and loyal husband, but he had become joyless and had taught their impressionable daughter that chasing beauty and popularity wasn't just a waste of time but also a character flaw. Her mother's character flaw. If this was Alice's second chance, she would try to undo some of the damage and teach Kaylee that life could also be fun.

Alice's heart beat sickeningly fast at the prospect of living with her daughter again, making dinner together, or just watching TV. Alice was ten minutes early when she arrived at the taco place, which was located in a rundown strip mall anchored by a dollar store and mattress store simply titled Mattress Warehouse. The parking lot was half empty, but the taco place was packed.

Before she stepped out of the car, Alice took a quick look at her makeup in the rearview mirror. Thankfully, her foundation and eyeliner didn't look like it was melting since it was much warmer in the Valley than the Westside, but the skin under her eyes had darkened, making her look tired, hollowed out. She took out a compact from her purse, flipped it open and caked the moist powder onto a tiny white sponge.

As she was applying the concealer, she jumped when she heard someone rapping at her window. Alice turned and saw her daughter standing outside. She snapped the compact shut, and got out to hug Kaylee.

"How are you?" she exclaimed, embracing her now adult daughter in her arms, rather than cradling Kaylee's tiny body against her chest as she had twenty-one years ago. Alice willed herself not to cry. It was not time to cry. They would celebrate her birthday, and perhaps a new beginning.

"All right," Kaylee said, seeming distracted even as she looked straight at her mother.

Alice noticed her hair didn't appear to have grown out at all in the three months since the funeral. In fact, it looked shorter and choppier, as if she'd cut her hair herself. This time, Kaylee hid her figure under a dark teal polo shirt and jeans instead of the gray frock at the funeral, where Alice only saw her from afar. Now she saw clearly just how much Kaylee resembled her father. Alice had always felt it was a shame that her daughter didn't inherit the natural crease of her eyelids but rather his single-lidded eyelids. Not only had he passed on his austere lifestyle, but also his weak chin and thin lips now imprinted on her daughter's face.

"The taco place is busy right now," Alice said. "That must mean it's really good, but do you want to go somewhere else less crowded, where we can sit down?"

Kaylee shrugged, and Alice felt a bit of hope.

"The mattress place is here, so we can go there first," Kaylee said.

Alice nodded, and they walked over to Mattress Warehouse, which looked abandoned, with black windows painted over by giant bubbly letters. Kaylee pushed the door, and it opened to an air-conditioned showroom, a maze of soft white slabs, dozens of them under beams of fluorescent lights. Only a couple of senior citizens were there when they walked in.

A woman with dyed orange hair instantly greeted them. A tag that read "The Proof is in Our Padding" was pinned to her black tank top just left of her cleavage. Kaylee gave her the model number for a mattress, and the saleswoman said she would check. When she turned to walk to the back of the store, she revealed a pair of large angel wings tattooed across her back from shoulder to shoulder. Alice looked at Kaylee to see if she had noticed, and whether it conjured up any memories of her father. Kaylee sat down on the nearest mattress, as if the encounter had already tired her out.

Kaylee's posture hadn't changed over the years. Her father would never say anything, if he even noticed her hunching over. Alice regretted not being there for her daughter's teenage years. She was not proud to admit she'd stayed away because her ex-husband had made her feel shallow and inadequate, but that was the truth. For Kaylee's sixteenth birthday, Alice offered to pay for surgery to add that missing crease to her eyelids, a common procedure that Asian girls would undergo to appear more approachable. Her ex-husband yelled at her for wanting to put their daughter's tender face under a knife. Framed like that, yes, Alice was a monster, but she had made the gesture out of love, because this world would be kinder to Kaylee if she could make some concessions to the world. Was Alice so horrible for looking out for her?

Kaylee still would not look at her, and seemed more interested in examining her nails than having a conversation.

"Are you buying a mattress for your dorm?" Alice asked as casually as she could, lest she give her daughter reason to draw up her defenses.

"I'm a senior so they don't allow us to live in dorms anymore," Kaylee said.

"So where are you living?" Alice asked.

"I rented a studio near campus. I just moved in, and it's unfurnished."

Alice couldn't have asked for a better opening to make her offer, imagining Kaylee living by herself in a sad, drab one-room box. At the same time, she was too chicken to ask her own daughter to live with her. She had to go about it in a less direct way.

"My friend has an apartment in Santa Monica," Alice began. "It's rent-controlled and only twelve hundred a month. I'm sure she can let you take it over if you want."

Her daughter finally looked up at her. Though Kaylee's expression might have appeared neutral to any stranger walking by, it could also be interpreted as pleased, maybe even happy.

"That's insanely cheap," Kaylee said.

"Yeah, my friend's moving to Florida," Alice lied. She should have told her she came with the deal, but wanted to see her daughter excited for a little while longer.

"It's only five blocks from the beach and the Promenade," Alice continued. "You can inhale the salt air from the ocean day and night."

"Why don't you take it?" Kaylee asked just as the saleswoman returned.

"I'm sorry, we don't carry that model anymore, but we have this new line," she said, pointing to the tag pinned to her shirt. "We have a test bed that you can choose from twenty-five comfort levels for your perfect night's sleep. Come and let me show you."

Alice and Kaylee followed the saleswoman's tattooed angel wings to a giant king-sized mattress as thick as two mattresses, one stacked on top of the other. The saleswoman picked up a remote control and asked Kaylee to lie down. She hesitated, but eventually took off her navy Converse sneakers, crawled across the bed on all fours and lay on her stomach.

"So just tell me if you want it softer or firmer," the saleswoman said, as Alice stood at the foot of the bed near her daughter's socked feet.

Alice could see the faintest outline of Kaylee's waist under the polo shirt abruptly spreading out into her hips. Was she getting enough exercise? And now Kaylee was pressing her cheek and mouth to a mattress that hundreds of people had rubbed up against.

"It's too soft right now, make it firmer," Kaylee said, her voice muffled.

"You're lying on your stomach," Alice said. "Wouldn't you gauge it better if you were lying on your back?"

The saleswoman motioned to Alice.

"Do you want to lay on it and test it too? There's plenty of room," she said.

"Sure," Alice said and slipped out of her strappy metallic sandals. She saw Kaylee lifting her head slightly toward the saleswoman. Was she mouthing something to her?

"Ready?" the saleswoman asked, after Alice had painstakingly inched her body toward her side of the mattress while trying to keep her sundress from riding up.

She eyed Kaylee who was motionless, as if she were playing dead. Once Alice was lying still on the bed, the top layer of the mattress seemed to instantly form a molded cushion around her body. She nodded at the saleswoman.

"Ready," she said.

That was when Kaylee said "firmer" and then repeated the word, almost like a chant. The bed began to harden, so much so that Alice thought she could feel every sharp edge of her body, the bones of her ankles, the points of her elbows and shoulder blades grating against the surface. Yet Kaylee kept asking for the bed to get even harder, and Alice's heart started to race as sickeningly fast as when she first arrived.

"Stop it," Alice said. "It's like a piece of wood now. Go back to what it was, make it softer."

"That's the firmest level," the saleswoman said.

Kaylee still didn't stir, so Alice couldn't catch her eye. What had happened to her daughter that she didn't think she deserved a nice soft bed? Had her father done this to her? Or was this Alice's doing?

"You can't have a bed like this," Alice exclaimed.

"I'll take the twin at the highest level of firmness," Kaylee said. Then she sprang up into a sitting position, out of Alice's reach.

"For two hundred more, you can get a full size," the saleswoman said, "and for three hundred more, you can get a queen."

"That's a great idea," Alice said, trying to sound upbeat even as she was looking over at the empty white space next to her. Just beyond it was Kaylee sitting on the bed.

"The room in Santa Monica can hold a queen easy," Alice kept talking when Kaylee didn't respond. "I'll pay for the mattress, so you don't have to worry about cost."

"I want a twin at this level of firmness," Kaylee repeated herself slowly and deliberately, with a harder edge to her voice. Clearly, she had made up her mind, and it scared Alice.

"Think of it as an investment for when your relationship status changes," the saleswoman said.

"Exactly," Alice said, grateful for the backup. "We'll take the queen, but please can we go down a few levels, otherwise no one else can sleep on it."

The saleswoman nodded, but Kaylee wouldn't back down. She stood up from the bed and took out her credit card before Alice could take hers out.

"Please give me what I asked for, or I'll walk out," she warned the saleswoman, whose smile wavered for the first time. Alice could only see Kaylee's back and not her face, but suspected she'd gone too far.

"I'll be right back," the saleswoman said, walking away with her daughter's card.

Kaylee didn't move, still standing with her back to her mother.

"Forget about the mattress, let me take you out to lunch," Alice said, sitting up on the bed. "If you like tacos, there's this great Cuban place in Venice, or we could go shopping at the Grove. We could buy new accessories and decorate our place."

"Our place?" Kaylee asked. "So you live there?"

Alice stiffened. Kaylee still hadn't turned around to face her.

"I do live there, and it's a wonderful apartment," Alice enthused, as if impersonating the saleswoman. "It has cute coffee shops everywhere, and there's a gym down the street. They have yoga and pilates classes and a trainer who comes in every week."

"Of course, it does," Kaylee said in a small voice.

"I feel energized after every session. Maybe we can go together, you and me."

"Live with you," Kaylee said, but it wasn't a question. Her shoulders trembled slightly, and then she bent her head down as if in prayer and buried her face in her open hands. Alice wanted to go to her, but couldn't move. She couldn't tell whether Kaylee was laughing or crying. She wanted to pry her daughter's hands from her face, as if she could glimpse at the woman Kaylee would become, but all she could see was a little girl resenting her, not letting her in.

Alice had a feeling they wouldn't be having lunch that day. And soon she would have to interview more potential roommates, so settled in their ways they would certainly be impossible to live with. Maybe then, Alice could invite Kaylee over and show her what could happen if she wasn't careful.

Mourning Missing Dopamine

By LI YUN ALVARADO

From Raising Mothers

Cuando estoy hasta las rodillas en ropa sucia y mi memoria,
nadie se preocupa de mi titulo: Directora Ejecutiva
del Hogar. Manejo los pantalones de yoga con faja de control,
los horarios, los trastes, y el bebé. Lo que le falta a esta organización
en metas y estratégias de hacer planes
a largo plazos, lo compensa en siestas y carreras contra el tiempo

The baby cries. The washer dings. I separate time
like dirty clothes. Endless days. My memory
spins like you, Papito. You danced spontaneity. Plans?
Ha! You never cared for the title: "Chief Executive
Officer of Your Life." Embrace the chaos, no? *Organization*
can wait another day, Mami, you'd say. *Everything's under control.*

La ropa sucia me diagnostica. Tan sencilla. Tan fuera de control:
Montón tras aburrido montón. Semana tras aburrida semana.Tiempo
ordena, fija, arranca, gira, agita, almacena. Desorganizadas,
las espumas bailan en el tambor húmedo. ¿Quién necesita memoria
funcional? Yo, lavando para cuatro, eso es quién. Asistente ejecutiva
imaginaria llena mis sueños. *Ella* si sabe hacer planes.

I lose the thread. Here. Gone. Papito, so many broken plans.
So many unbought plane tickets. Nothing under control.
We all help. I take the paperwork. Good executive,
eldest daughter. There's clothing to wash, but time
hangs. *Papi, meet my son, your namesake. Cling to his memory.*
Goodbye? My life: disordered. It doesn't exist: organization.

Bomba y plena. Procesión. Tierra húmeda. Después, organizo
mi hogar. Elimino alboroto, ropa, hasta los libros. Hago planes.
Cancelo. El tocayo recién nacido amamanta recuerdos y memoria.
Iniciar la tarea? No puedo comenzar. No dejo de comenzar. ¿Control
de impulsos? Tíralo todo. Compra más. ¿Emocional? El tiempo:
despliega, gira, se escurre. ¿Autocontrol? No evalúo ni termino. No sirvo de Ejecutiva.

Function? How inflexible! How emotional! My executive
function won't function. Mourning missing dopamine. In school, organization
came easier. I could play those school rhythms. Knew how to keep time
to those beats. You and me, afternoons and weekends full of plans.
You'd arrive on your bike or on foot. If we're talking fun, it's all under control.
Now what? Laundry and raising grandfatherless grandkids. My memory,

mi herencia. También esta (dis)función ejecutiva. Today I spin plans,
shake out organization. Easy Papito, everything (more or less) under control.
Doblo las camisas tuyas de los viejos tiempos. I nuzzle your namesake, guardian of memory.

Flight

Adapted from The Wild Swans *by Hans Christian Andersen*

by DÉSIRÉE ZAMORANO

This itching at my back is maddening. Nights have been unbearable for sleep, with this ferocious itching, with my skin at the edge of fire, so I leave my husband, the King, and find comfort in the antechamber, where Kjirste, my servant, waits. I send her to fetch the salve and she disappears.

I fear the incessant itching and back-numbing scratching is a punishment from a god I stopped believing in the moment the Archbishop bent down to light the pyre built around me. And when the flames transformed into poppies, I laughed at the glorious power of magic!

This all sounds chaotic and mad, I'm not telling things in the right order, in my mind they are not in the right order, they are all at once. A child with her brothers; a mute sixteen-year-old girl staring at her pyre; a queen, lying here, waiting desperately for her servant. Let me try to card the threads of truth from this lump of memories.

Years ago, when I was a child, my brothers and I had gold slates with diamond pencils. My favourite picture book cost half the kingdom. From that time with my brothers I can only remember sunshine and green leaves: I was their beloved. They spoiled and protected and loved me. I never knew my mother, and I did not feel the lack.

My father, the King, and my true mother had twelve children. What do you suppose they were imagining? But really, what was my father thinking? Of course it was going to all end in tears; it was as if my father thought, how many births will it take to break my mother? Twelve. Mine.

Naturally, my father remarried.

I remember thinking at their wedding how old and cruel she was, his bride, my stepmother, the new Queen. (In my dream last night she murmured something to me, what was it? Just before the maddening itching at my back woke me.) The truth was the new Queen was very beautiful, in that grown-up, sophisticated manner of a woman who has been with men who desired her.

People blamed the stepmother. I certainly did—so much simpler to blame a cunning woman than a besotted man. So much easier to complain that he is being lied to, deceived, toyed with, when the fact is he's too boorish to care about his own children.

He certainly never noticed that she did not like my brothers at all.

***

She wore a fabulous robe which had arrived from across the seas. The lace trim alone was said to have blinded scores of poor French girls. My fifth brother, Erling, provoked her for the very last time by pouring his porridge on her throne seat. Unknowingly, she sat in the puddle of congealed mush and damaged her mantle.

She insisted that all the brothers be brought to the main hall. Throughout the night, she demanded to know who had done this terrible thing. I hid under the main table, and I bit my fist as I watched my stepmother, now without a cloak, dark and furious, pacing before my eleven brothers, standing from youngest to oldest, mute. Some angrily contemptuous, like Ansgar, the oldest, flashing his eyes at her as she passed. None of them would ever betray their brother. Uffe, who never had any sense, barely hid his laughter behind his thick, pink hands.

"Done," she said, responding to his chortles and the dawn in the distance.

"What was done," I wailed, and in that instant my brothers turned into swans and flew out the window. I choked on my surprise, my terror, my fright. I felt the horror, and the abandonment.

It wasn't until I found them much later, that I learned they returned to human form at night.

***

My dreams have me thinking quite a bit about my stepmother. How clever she was, what power to change my brothers into swans. If only she had chosen me!

***

Well-told by the common folk, and indeed a true story, was how I was banished from my father's sight. My stepmother stained my skin with walnut juice until I was as brown as a Moor. My father looked at me in horror and declared I was no flesh of his. That sent me on my journey to join my brothers.

(What the common folk do not tell is the strange way my father had begun to look at me; the way he nervously licked at his dry lips when he visited me, alone in my room, the way my flesh felt thick and strange when he pawed at it. Had she known? Was that her way of shielding me?)

***

Where is Kjirste? She has probably fallen asleep, but I have no pity for her. She is seventeen and very pretty and the menservants swirl about her. My husband smiles at her, the way he smiled at me when I was young and mute, more than a dozen years ago.

***

Dreams guided my search for my brothers; dreams led me off on foot and through pain and peril until I found them, and the twelve of us fell into each other's arms, weeping and embracing.

In the morning they swept me up in their wings. I have known but one flight, to this kingdom, where my eleven swan brothers carried me over the swirling sea, through the threatening sky. I was too frightened to enjoy the pleasure of the wind, then I was too terrified to do anything but close my eyes and pray, as that was how I had been taught. I prayed and wept, blind to the world around me.

Idiot girl.

Deposited in this land, again, dreams guided me, and elaborated on what I would have to do to free my brothers: gather nettles, card the stinging plants into slivers of threads, spin the threads into yarn, knit eleven sweaters, and never utter a single word until those sweaters were complete.

Then my brothers' lives were so precious to me, they were all I knew, all my world. I shredded, carded, then knit into the evenings. This, after having cooked their food and readied their home for their flights as swans at dawn, at dusk they returned whole and surrounded and comforted and cared for me. But they could not answer my questions as my dreams forbade me from speaking.

I could only use nettles that were grown on gravestones. Stinging nettles. My lips bled as I bit them, to keep myself from uttering cries of pain and lamentation.

As I gathered, carded, spun and knit, I developed a new appreciation for my stepmother. She was actually quite impressive. Imagine transforming eleven young men into swans. What power! What majesty!

At times I still can feel the pain of the nettles' stinging, while I was forbidden to cry out. As I've told my husband many, many times—once I was prohibited from talking, and now you will not shut me up!

One cannot endure a year of finger-burning nettle-picking, carding then knitting in complete and utter silence without having gleaned some talents. When the King of this land encountered me, spinning, spinning, spinning, I smiled and, without uttering a word, gained shelter, gained his protection.

I continued to seek nettles grown on gravestones, continued to knit the sweaters that would permanently return my brothers to the bodies God had given them. The King of this country indulged me.

***

Tonight it is as if the nettles have returned, have entered through my finger tips and now prick me all over, just underneath my skin. My skin burns with the sticking of small needles, but most terribly at my back.

***

The Archbishop hated me. Or did he long for me? In either case he plotted against me, denounced me to this King as a witch, exhorted the mob who raved at me, and eagerly set the pyre under my feet alight. As speaking would doom my brothers to live permanently as swans, I could not utter a word in my defense. When the Archbishop raised his torch, as the kingdom watched, I flung the sweaters (one still missing a sleeve) up to the heavens and my swan brothers flew into their sweaters and transformed back into men.

Was that not witchcraft? Was not the Archbishop, who resented me, correct? The flames transformed into red poppies (more witchcraft); my benefactor, the King, plucked one and presented its redness to me, and I fainted. The common folk said it was from love.

Love?

People, I was mightily exhausted! I had just travelled the universe of my passions—I hadn't said a single word of assent to my now husband, the king, and apparently all a woman has to do to acquiesce is to be silent!

We were wed that afternoon. The entire town cheering and celebrating, having anticipated a conflagration now drunk on the spectacle of my brothers, the swans—no, now my brothers, the Princes, followed by more drinking and marvelling, and me, dumb, not by choice now, but by shock.

For months after the wedding, the entire country it seemed would visit, to take a gander at the woman whose life was one long entertainment for the realm. My brothers all settled into this kingdom. I thought they should be acrobats, and go on tour with actors, but, no. They demanded land and titles from my husband–and found fat round wives who giggled a lot and gave them each plenty of babies.

***

I have had no babies and I do not giggle. Well, not unless it is at the sight of my husband-when he is naked.

***

When my husband learned the full story of my brothers' enchantment, what did he do? With the subtlety of a mad boar, he and his armies tracked my stepmother down. The Archbishop supervised her pyre himself.

I was, of course, not consulted. I was, of course, presumed to be in the flattering role of grateful girl. I was, instead, not innocent but incandescent.

Indeed, those thoughts had been what had kept me carding those nettles, despite the pain that shot through my fingertips, my arms, my body. How had this woman been so powerful?

Karin, my servant before Kjirste, told me my stepmother was neither burned nor buried. She was nowhere to be found when my husband's army appeared before my father's-castle. That what was burned instead was a poor effigy.

That was when the new dreams began. When my stepmother whispered to me in my sleep.

***

What had she told me last night? I reach out, and her words disappear.

Holy Trinity, my back is in flames! The skin of my arms filled with prickles, my legs needled with pain. Everything burns. Childbirth could not be worse. I yell for Kjirste.

***

Months after the wedding, when I had words back in my mouth, I asked my brothers, over and over and over again what it was like to fly, to soar, to swim in the air—and they mumbled and instead talked of other things.

They could go anywhere they chose! And yet they remained here. I am constrained by the castle, by the kingdom, by my husband, the King.

They really are a boring lot.

My brothers–aren't bad men. Their peasants are fed, their women unmolested. They're not particularly good or interesting men, either. They have servants to do the daily work, wives to have their babies. They happily put their heavy feet up on stools and smile at their patch of land, all very smug and pleased with themselves, as if achieved by their own exertions. Their sister married well, I can tell you!

I am done with them all, and find any manner of pretext to avoid their invitations to their christenings, feast days, name days, holidays. They hint very heavily about invitations to the castle, and on that score I do not mind as much. I sit at the head table with my husband the King and gaze down at them.

And think, all that pain for this?

Let's face it, if I had depended on the eleven of them for a single knit sweater, this story would have ended very differently.

***

My skin burns! The itch right under both my shoulder blades is maddening! Precisely where I cannot reach.

***

My brother, Throvald, gave me a drawing he had done of myself from that time, when I was said to be the cause of all my stepmother's misery, more than a dozen years ago. I was as pale as a worm from under a rock! I was wan and dull; the common folk said I was filled with innocence and goodness.

I was insipid.

I complied quite a lot. I think of that now, often. Now I say no for the perversity of it.

My brothers are a disappointment.

Except Hans, our youngest brother. He flew into the unfinished sweater and he holds his wing-close to him. I cannot tell if he is fearful of losing feathers or embarrassed by their presence. He did not demand land or a wife. He has taken up as a gameskeeper. He keeps to himself. He's inordinately generous to his manservant. While the other brothers bore me to tears, he worries me. I do not know how he makes his way in this world, and he disappears for hours and hours, my Kjirste tells me.

Where does he go? What does he do?

How does he manage to disappear for hours? Could he not at least share that secret with me?

***

In the first dream of my stepmother, she was dressed completely in pristine white fur, her dark hair spilling out from underneath her hat. Her eyes and mouth hinted at amusement.

She said, "How did I not see?" I yearn for her visits in my dreams. What did she whisper to me in my dreams last night? It has slipped away.

Just now, when I lay on my bed, face down, Kjirste started to rub the cream onto my bare back, gave a little shriek, dropped the pot of salve and ran out. I demanded that she return. She covered her face with her apron and told a terrible story about something growing under my skin. I threatened to cut out her tongue should I hear even a whisper of what she said.

***

Kjirste is gone, I cannot find her. I hear the morning doves coo in anticipation of the dawn. I remove my night robe, my night dress, and press my back against the cold stone floor. The burning is momentarily quelled. I can breathe peacefully again.

From where I lay I can see the sky moving from grey to pink. I rise to the window, the air that enters cools and calms me. I concentrate on the ribbon of colour to distract me from the pain. The grey cast to the sky is disappearing; rose skims the undersides of the clouds. Dawn was when my brothers became swans.

I stand on the window ledge to better watch. The sun explodes—I am in flames! Only the cool rush of air will soothe me. I know now what my step-mother whispered—"Come," she said. I step from the window ledge to join her at last, and soar east, in the direction of the sun.

mother tongue

by DILYS WYNDHAM THOMAS

my mother would leave envelopes on my pillow   letters of
erasure   not of apology

ma petite chérie

in French   a butterfly can also be a moth   and to heal a wound
is to cure what caused it   in its corridors of imperative moods
and silent endings   truth talks in conditionals   the written word
deciphers what the heart cannot perceive

le coeur ne parle pas anglais

i tried to write back using the songs that she sang   the rhythms
that she wore   the cries she muffled behind closed doors   but I
could never carry a tune   in their mother tongue   some words
are too heavy to be set down   to be bilingual is to be tongue-tied
hands behind your back

les mots se perdent

that first poem started as a letter when she left without a word
airmail paper that smelt of petrol and perfume   of roses not
knotted around her neck   but the hurt bloomed into questions
and questions into verse   and the questions had a power that
only verse understood   absence makes the heart grow thorns

alors   pourquoi

every year   my mother sent us autumn leaves in the post   oak
and crumpled ash   echoes of rot and rainfall   in French
there is a single word for both solitude and loneliness   no border
crossing from privacy to intimacy no modern word for petrichor

ce dictionnaire de non-dits

we talked with her on the landline   my sister and i   waiting
in line   staying in line   toeing the line   until   down the
line   we barely speak   five minutes a week   a fortune in
words unsaid

un mur de paroles

three decades on   I let my french wilt and go to seed   I will
no longer speak the ache stuck in my throat   in my mother's
tongue sadness and sorrow are twins   not cousins   so I write
in a language she will never understand   poems of erasure   not
of apology

il ne reste plus rien à dire

Hawksong

by HAZEL KIGHT WITHAM

Today, after blast of kidrage into quiet quarantine morning, I leave my home to run out my anger.

I fly to the corner of my block, abandoning small relentless humans. I look up, and on perch of telephone pole a hawk side-eyes me as he tears into breakfast, feathers fluttering from his beak, lilting ruin.

The hawk screeches through his meal, kee-yahing hawksong into day. I wonder if he sees threat as I stand below transfixed, spell-bound by suburban wildness.

I watch for minutes. He keeps crying to me, shrilling his hunger, his grief, his anger.

I boil with him. Rip tendons, rend flesh, spit feathers. My hawk-self wants to shred morning too, so I run, pound concrete earth, and try to be free of the life I am so lucky to live.

...

One month before pandemic stopped all the clocks, we moved back into my spacious childhood home, in a neighborhood I thought I was done with.

The home my moms remodeled in late eighties style, though I never understood how lesbians could choose rose and almond tiles for their master bath.

When Mom #2, my bonus mom, my mom of calm, died of a brutal, belligerent cancer, the big home was a bit too empty for Mom #1, and so we began dreaming of building her a small house in the back, and transforming the front house for my family of four.

Now, we are here, having built this dream and moved into it February, 2020. My mom is 44 steps away, her dog and cat no doubt puzzled by the downsizing.

Now everything has stopped, except my gratitude at the spaciousness where we can all lose our minds together.

...

The last time I lost the world, most everyone else went on as usual.

My second born arrived with galloping shock, scorching my underappreciated normal, both our systems on brink of collapse. Severe pre-eclampsia. I listened as his swift heartbeat rhythmed across four days of hospital lockdown.

Four days—small hospital eternity. I did not know if we would make it out.

Uncertainty staccatoed the space between every *bah-bum* pounding his *still alive* soundtrack.

I flailed for something solid to ground me and my sky-high anxiety. All my beloveds kept our once-shared world turning while swimming boy and I hunkered down, tended by the best of strangers and their choreographed care.

Everything stopped, stilled, save my frantic brain trying to take back the reins in that room we could not leave.

When he came, he would stay in the Neonatal Intensive Care Unit for 82 days, and every day I would visit. Holding him in the small clutch of hours, skin-to-skin, breathing together through each lucky present moment kept me sane.

...

We drifted through the early grateful years with our miracle boy, astonished at how far he had come, amused by his strong opinions and refusal to cry it out. When he needed us in the middle of the night, he did not fuss, or drift gently back to sleep. He screamed to bring down the house. We lifted his small body. We soothed, we sang "*only fools rush in*," we marveled at his resilience.

Those days of grateful blessing and baby wonder are gone. I wake most quarantine mornings to screaming from the boy who was born one pound, ten ounces. Now forty pounds and fury: he cannot do all that others can, cannot have all that others have. He has lost his teachers, his friends, his pre-k life, all the good routines. His hunger, his grief, his anger, launch us into day.

...

It is a family of Cooper's hawks. Four of them. They nested in the massive sycamore reigning outside my bedroom window. Now they afternoon in the pepper tree in our neighbor's yard, silencing songbirds, eyeing the dog who splays in the sun as her days slow.

I hear one calling that forsaken cry, the telephone pole war-song I heard during breakfast of bird.

I keep gendering the hawk male, though I know many fierce women.

Anger is my father's language. War-making, battle-planning. I am in my mothers' house, place of peace, refuge. These last months, as my three males and I moved in, it has heard more screaming than the past four decades.

But right now it is blessedly quiet, the boys have gone with their dad, yet I still feel lost and lonely as I tear into this one hour of sustenance. Like the hawk wailing even as he fed, I am in such a frequent state of grief and overwhelm, that my free time, my precious alone time, is soaked in desperation.

I need the view of the hawk—the wide lens, the open sky, the ability to look far into future—some scream-free, screen-free, virus-less time when we can hold people we love who do not live with us. When will that be?

...

I wonder sometimes if my boy's anger came when he was a 28-week baby, starved to 26-week size in my inhospitable womb. I wonder if I now feel anger I did not express then—when tiny boy shuddered the world to a halt so we both could survive.

I remember the doctor who stopped me a week after my earlybird was born when I was on my way out of the NICU to say how much better I looked, now that I was no longer pregnant and tethered to life by magnesium and IVs. She said, as so many said, "It's good you came in when you did."

And this: "You were 24 hours away from disaster for one or both of you."

...

Some days his yelling renders me Arctic: Victor Frankenstein sledging across ice floes, fleeing his impossible Creation.

Mary Shelley delivered her first baby premature, at seven months in February 1815. Her baby died two weeks later, leaving Mary bereft and horrified at the grief that can accompany motherhood.

I learn this fact after I had my second baby premature at six months in February 2015, exactly 200 years after Mary. My Creation lives thanks to science and nurses and doctors, but my second motherhood, forged in trauma, fired first in NICU lockdown then COVID quarantine, often renders me monstrous, a creator unrecognizable to myself.

...

My moms' dog will be dead soon, her body a story of bones today as we said our goodbyes.

Today my earlybird reads a 400-page book though his five-year-old brain does not process written words just yet. After he turns all the pages he is proud to announce he's "read the whole book."

I want to know what reading means when it is sea of things you cannot decipher, senseless waves of black lines across white expanse. What does anger mean when it sears through me, threatening who I think I am?

What does dying, watching dying, become, as virus slaughters our loved ones, asks the unthinkable of hospital workers, and all those who remain bear breathless witness.

How do we read this inscrutable time? How will we?

...

The hawks have vanished. They didn't take me with them.

There is something humming inside me I do not want to name. Today I write in pencil and refuse to leave the house.

My tears hold no answers. My small boy brings a clear glass of cold water. From the beginning he has asked me to be present, to be with him, here, now.

My mom told me once that depression is anger turned inward. I keep using the word quicksand, keep trying to describe the hollowing as something else—this hopeless echo of that hospital time when world was a tidal wave of fear, and I did not know if my boy and I would survive.

The sun paws my shoulder, mugging the overcast of day. I look out at the empty trees.

Somewhere the hawk finishes its meal, some newly silent thing, talon-clenched, still, save for the way the sharp maw of ferocity keeps rending its body into offering.

The Poet's Corrido

After Frida Kahlo's *The Dream (The Bed)*

by XOCHITL-JULISA BERMEJO

"I had the strangest dream," she says not asking
permission to continue. "I'm in my bed,
but it's not my bed." This is how all dream retellings
begin. "I'm flying through the sky!" She means

floating in clouds. She does not yet have the word
for *tree* or for how it entombs her body in leaves.
Death is in the dream, but she won't name him.
His femurs are bound by explosives. She's losing

time and decides her marigold blanket is "a gold cape
weaved for a warrior." She writes *lavender lilies*
on a piece of parchment. But the ticking still ticks.
Details mix. "Sharks hunt the heavens!" From bed,

she pens *door handle, knock, unlock*. Open
possibility for the poet sprouting roots from toes.

Ritual of Wholeness

by XOCHITL-JULISA BERMEJO

Yellow lemons grew ripe
behind her house,
and when I was younger,
but no longer little,
I would speed past her
working in the kitchen, barely
a hello, out the back door,
to select a single, bright Myer.
Grandma stayed silent
as I carried the fruit in, laid it
at the counter, bared the knife,
sliced it through the belly.
Not until we were seated
at the table, she watching
from across the way
as I squeezed and spilled juice
over a bowl of tender frijoles
swimming in caldo, not until
I devoured two healthy helpings,
did she say with a wink,
"¿Porque no comes? ¿No tienes
hambre?" As if to say, want
could never be shameful.

Letter from a Grieving Mother

by ERIKA AYÓN

I remember the water. It kept coming. I remember
reaching for my daughter and husband. My arms
almost grasping theirs, catching my breath,
seeing them sinking below. The Rio Brava
has claimed so many lives. It was dangerous
to cross this way. We wanted a better life.
For our daughter to grow up with freedom,
feeling like she could do anything. Knowing
that a woman has rights. To never, like me,
be assaulted by her boss. To be held down,
threatened to be killed, if she told anyone,
a knife pressed against her neck, shaking.
We wanted to protect our daughter.
For her to never feel afraid for her life
because she was a woman. To know she could fight.
I am sitting here at the edge of the river,
my daughter, my husband are lying face down
on the dirt. She's wearing a red sweater.
He's wearing a blue shirt. I am yelling
their names, no one can hear me.
I am haunted by who they were before this.
How quickly a person can leave the living.
How quickly I went from holding her hand,
caressing her cheeks, whispering stories in her ear.
How quickly all was lost.
I will carry them with me. Relive the what ifs.
What if we took a different route? Waited another day,

another second to jump into the river?
Is it possible to barter with the river,
to give my life for theirs?
Can I tend to the river
in exchange for their souls?
Water terrifies me now,
even a drop makes me gasp for air.

Ammama's Garden

by SUHASINI YEEDA

There's a photo of you in your garden—one arm behind your back, one in front balanced on the garden gate, holding a pair of scissors. You're in the middle of talking to me, though I can't recall what about. You're smiling as you speak.

This was the morning of your 90th birthday. You woke early, had a cup of Lipton black tea with half a packet of Splenda. You fed your mini poodle, Splinter. You did your morning exercise—reaching up high, bending down to touch your toes, then walking from the garage door to the dining room repeating the movement multiple times.

I watched as you marched in your chappals with purpose. I met you in your garden where you had already begun pruning dried up bits. You told me that the plants, the flowers needed pruning otherwise they'd never grow.

Your hair was stark white, disheveled, and full. You swore by that blue and white bottle of coconut oil. You wore your nightgown while gardening, the royal blue one with a bright pink floral pattern.

When I look at this photo, I see a very different grandma than the one I remember from my childhood. Happier, lighter, more free perhaps.

In my childhood, you had salt and pepper hair and less smile lines around your eyes, but the physical changes of aging aren't what has made you so different. You lived right down the street from us, and I came over often, but I never really got to know you or let you get to know me. We knew each other only from what my mom said. I had a limited understanding of you because of this and I can only assume the same applied to you.

As a child, I admit, I was a little scared of you. You seemed so serious, righteous, even antiquated at times. I suppose someone 60 years older than me is bound to be a little old fashioned.

What I remember of my grandmother from my childhood was one who argued with my mom about how she was too lenient with her "American" kids, how her husband, my dad, was always not measuring up to her expectations. Mom married a lesser caste when she married my father. She was from the Kshatriya caste, and he was from Vaishyas caste. Still, my grandparents thought it was a good match because my dad was also Christian and because he had a brilliant engineer brother in the U.S. who could supply a safe landing place for my mother's potential American Dream.

Before my dad, before me and my sibling were born, mom already had resentments. She always felt like she was second in line—especially to the two siblings of hers who were sent to college. Mom argued that she should have gone too. Once, she even located her primary and secondary school report cards to prove the fact to me. I heard this complaint more times than I can recall. Eventually like many family affairs—her opinion became lodged in my brain, and it sat there at the center of all things Ammama—you were clearly the bad guy, grandma. But when I look at this photo, that isn't who I see.

The morning of your 90th birthday, you walked around your garden full of rose bushes, chrysanthemums, vines full of jasmine, mint and curry leaf bushes. You snipped bendekai, brinjal, and tomatoes, showing me proudly how large they came out.

This wasn't your first garden. I'm not even sure it is your second, but it is the second one I've known. You don't live in the home I spent my childhood anymore—the one with a granny smith apple tree that I thought was named "granny" because you had grown them. You grew watermelons larger than any grocery store sold. Crape myrtle trees with pink fuzzy blooms adorned your front yard. That home had a large swing set in the backyard, where I first made belief with my neighbor friends. With each swing, we were transported to far off lands, to planets, to the moon, to wherever this wooden rocket ship would carry us.

I remember that house well. When I went away to college at the end of my sophomore year, you moved further north, leaving our neighborhood and my mother behind. She definitely took this personally. This was a white flight pattern many Indian Americans took as an effort to distance themselves from uptick in the Black and Latinx residents after the effects of Hurricane Katrina. I was learning this term "white flight" in college right around the time you moved, and I remember not being surprised that you had joined the pack of Indians that wanted to remain assimilated to, approximate to white populations of Dallas.

The grandmother I grew up with sometimes said racist, sexist, and homophobic comments—a product of the influence of British colonialism you were born into, marrying a high ranking member of the British Indian Army, living a decade in pre-apartheid South Africa, and the thirty something years you'd live in the conservative Mesquite, Texas suburb we both once called home. I didn't even know three of the four lives you'd lived before you moved into the house down the street from my family. I wasn't born until three years after that move took place.

I can't recall a single time where I helped you with the vegetables in your garden at that old house. On your 90th birthday though—I held them in my hands and cleaned the dirt away, water from the kitchen faucet pouring over my fingertips. I felt the waxy brinjal skin become like silk, I enjoyed the fuzzy texture of the bendekai as it tickled my palms. Later that evening, I'd reap the rewards of your hard work by filling my plate with a mound of basmati rice and your vegetables—now transformed to homemade curries, chutney, and pickle.

Much like the flowers and vegetables in your garden that you promised only grew to their full potential when pruned, so too did you appear to become more fully yourself once widowed from my Tathi. It's hard to say which is the "real Ammama." Perhaps they both contain you. I can only say what I observed and that is that life pushed you to start again, to form a new identity outside of the man you'd been married to since you were a teenager.

You were independent, firm in your faith in God—not religious like the story of the money changers, merchants, and Pharisees in the Bible—but faithful and confident. You grew in ways that shocked me. I don't say that lightly. You stunned me, Ammama. You showed me that people aren't concrete, but malleable if they chose to soften themselves. You proved to me that the time old excuse of "she's of a certain generation" or "she's too old to change" was a bullshit excuse people used to validate the backwards behavior and opinions of their own grandparents.

But you angered me long before you inspired me. I was young, not yet born, when some things happened in our family, but I know you chose family above all. You chose your sons and didn't correct their wrongs—their wives isolated and in pain. But I didn't know these women then, nor had I developed a clear understanding of what abuse could look like, how the matriarch of a family could protect abusers because they were family.

I always thought "family first" made sense until the unfortunate day it applied to me. He was my cousin, he was family too, so you argued that we should not call the police or make a formal restraining order. I sat alone in my bedroom, only ten years old, as the adults made decisions about my life without me. I wished I had the courage of Jesus to "overthrow the tables" of the wicked Pharisees of my family.

A year after my mother passed away, you flew alone to New York to watch me walk the stage and earn my graduate degree. Not having any parents alive to celebrate, you made it a point to be there. Cane in hand, you, me, and my sister walked around the idyllic campus. I pointed out the flowers that lined the admission building, not knowing their names. You stuck your nose to the petals and breathed in their floral scent.

A few months later, I'd take you up on your offer to come stay at your house. I slept in the bedroom my mom stayed in before she went to the hospital for the last time. Sometimes, in the middle of the night I'd open the closet door and reach to the back where some of mom's clothes still hung. I'd pull her gray sweater to my nose and breathe in a swirl of Yardley lavender talcum powder and soft notes of Elizbeth Taylor's White Diamonds.

She passed away in early May. I came to stay with you one year and two months later, unsure of what to expect, not sure how long I'd stay, just seeking a much-needed rest after a year of withholding grief with the convenient excuse of school responsibilities.

You taught me how to cook and fold a saree the right way. You had almond milk waiting in the fridge so I could enjoy cereal with you in the morning. You cried in front of me and spoke highly of my mom, of how many immigrants she helped when they showed up in a brand-new unfamiliar country. You bragged to relatives about all the stories I had to "imagine" and "make" to earn my MFA. You tried to make sure my sister and I valued our relationship—stating more than once, you're all each other has now. You took care of me like I was your daughter. Sometimes, you'd become very serious in tone and tell me that I was your daughter now.

One day I sat in your living room sprawled out on the couch, half watching CNN with you, half lurking Twitter as the case of Obergefell v. Hodges resulted in the legalization of same-sex marriage in every state in the U.S. I looked at you, anticipating some pushback, some Biblical reason why you didn't support this. Not fully out yet, I sat very still and prepared myself for disappointment. You smiled at the screen and clapped. Without insulting, I wondered if you knew what you were cheering on and had to ask. "Grandma, do you know what these people are celebrating?" I asked meekly. "Yes." You paused. "They are all God's children. They deserve love too." I sat up and watched you cheering, and I joined you, surprised.

Another day you told me quietly that you were secretly sending small lumps of money to your niece in India so that she could escape an abusive relationship. You helped her with travel and secured a small flat where she could safely put her life back together. You'd ask me "look on your phone rupees to dollars conversion." Each time you asked, I was reminded that this knowledge was only needed so you could continue supporting this woman.

Years later, you called me while I was at work. You did this often, forgetting the time zone difference we now share. I always answered anyway, sneaking my way outside for privacy. It wasn't an accident. You knew you called during work this time. You wanted to tell me right away.

"He died." I didn't ask who. There was a noticeable silence between us. I walked further away from the building, prepared to end the silence with a question of who—but you continued. "He was living in India because he could not work in America anymore." She paused, allowing me time to let that fact sink in. "The police found him dead on the floor of his apartment with pills all around."

I didn't respond. I knew she was speaking about the cousin from when I was ten. I smiled instantly, because this evil man was gone from the earth, unable to harm anyone again. "I wanted to tell you as soon as I found out." She finished. I kept smiling. I was surprised that I was smiling. She'd never be able to undo her choices. She knew that, but she also knew the peace it would give me to know he was dead and she provided that right away, in her own way apologizing for not protecting me before.

The Ammama I knew as a child seemed stubborn and set in her ways. But when I came to her as an adult, orphaned, heartbroken, with no idea what to do next, she welcomed me in and proved me wrong. Not because she wasn't those things at some point. I was right. She was so serious, righteous, and even mean when I was younger.

But you, Ammama, are much like roses in your garden, you pruned and snipped away at yourself slowly, slowly so you could blossom again, anew.

You are 94 now and your garden is gone. Your health has not been strong enough to garden. The plants were dug up sometime when I was not there to witness its upheaval. I felt a sharp sadness when I sat in your living room on my first trip home after COVID, gazing out the window, surprised to see the dirt patches and grass that remained.

I sat next to you and looked down at your hands. They were much thinner and longer versions of my own. I told you that when my mother—your daughter—died, I couldn't look at my hands for months. They reminded me too much of hers. I told you I had vivid dreams of her where I sat and talked with her as if she'd never died. When I awoke, I became so angry because I felt like my mind had played some sort of trick on me. I was stuck, unpruned, frost-bitten by what life had given to me to endure.

You shared with me that you too had these kinds of dreams—of my mother, of your sister, of the many loved ones you had lost in your lifetime. You seemed sad, bittersweet, but never angry about these dreams.

You said plainly, "She came to visit me last night." Not that she had appeared. That she visited. You believed they were real which made me begin to listen closer to my dreams. You made me believe that I could look down at my hands, feel the breeze on my cheeks, shake myself free of my old leaves and start fresh.

When I close my eyes and imagine your garden, Ammama, it is just as it appears in this photo. You are standing proudly, smiling at the many fruits of your labor. The smell of jasmine and roses rush together, the taste of your vegetables dance on my tongue. I am transported.

Writing My Father's Journals

by LISA EVE CHEBY

A Hungarian immigrant enters a bar. Everyone toasts,
and he hears *bacsi!*, imagines his brother's hand on his shoulder.

His daughter, American, poet, enters a carpeted room. Everyone wields
fine plastic pens and are told: imagine something real

the smell of pickled meats
flies sipping drops of cherry-dew on pits
the rupture of each red drop

a balloon, a broken bottle. She tiptoes through the shards
of broken intentions and Kerouac dreams of what it means

to hope in America. She lies

on a bed in a solitary room and listens to ink penetrating the page,
a score of the days he didn't record

cruising in a 1959 Dodge Royal:
two-door, hardtop, black and chrome curves give way
to sharp angles glinting over open roads cutting
through landscapes of loneliness.

Signature

by ROZ WEISBERG

from Bangalore Review

The first letter of Georgia's name was supposed to be a tribute to a dead great-grandmother on her father's side that no one remembered. She'd always been grateful that despite her father's insistence, her mother refused to name her Gertrude which was the name of the deceased great-grandmother. When Georgia learned to write her name in cursive, she gave the "G" an extra swirl through the middle that looped across, its tail sweeping below the pale blue line on the wide-ruled paper in Mrs. Deal's third-grade class. Mrs. Deal marked the extra loop with a red felt pen, writing her own cursive G over Georgia's, demonstrating how the extra swirl made Georgia's "G" look like a "Q."

The middle line evolved. Georgia's silent act of defiance created a more dramatic and elaborate signature. Although she was right-handed, she tried to mimic her left-handed father's signature in order to forge notes to get out of gym class. His signature was compressed, jagged and difficult to read even before his tremors turned it into an EKG readout. The secretaries in the front office accepted the forgeries, choosing to believe her father must be a doctor.

She'd lost count of the documents she'd signed on his behalf over the past four years, though it was the first time the section required "next of kin" instead of "power of attorney". Sliding the clipboard back across the counter, the nurse stood up and peered through his reading glasses on the tip of his nose. His eyes rose above the rim of the lens as he spun the clipboard back around to face her and tapped the signature line, “Would you mind printing your name? We need to make sure it’s readable.”

Georgia accommodated and watched her hand move on its own through each letter with certainty. Her name seemed foreign on the consent forms switching her father’s care from life-saving to life-ending. The diaper brigade of residents predicted his passing would take a few hours, advising her to call whomever needed to be called. The nurse reached across, took the clipboard again, and skimmed the white spaces for marked boxes. “That’s better. Okay. Do you have a DNR or advanced directives? They don’t seem to be in his files.”

Without answering, she found the manila envelope she’d shoved in her backpack when she’d got the call from the assisted living facility that he’d gone to the hospital. She handed the neon pink DNR over before flipping through the blue backed legal documents that included his advance directives. His initials were scratched into the cream colored double bonded paper next to each instruction. The palliative section requested that pain or discomfort be alleviated even if it caused death. She hadn’t remembered reading that before.

Georgia traced her finger over the ballpoint depression of her father’s signature, unable to recognize the letters under her fingertips, until the nurse eased the documents away.

Sexual Habits of African American Teen Girls: Unauthorized data collection by some white male doctor, February 1974

by ASHTON CYNTHIA CLARKE

Even through the twisting pain, my concern was ruining the cloth seats of my neighbor's green Gremlin as she chauffeured me to the emergency room of Bronx Municipal Hospital. My violent uterine contractions were not producing life, just dead issuance of crimson, maroon, and bloodclaat brown. I was in agony from another hellish monthly period.

Begging for some caring contact, I reached for my father sitting next to me in the back seat. But the sheepskin-gloved hands folded in his lap offered little in the way of comfort. Eventually, my head flopped to one side, resting on Daddy's shoulder. He continued to stare straight ahead, silent, and unmoving, as if mortified by my moaning display of weakness and his own cringeworthy situation.

So why was Daddy accompanying me on the ultimate in women's problems? Perhaps Mommy was suffering in bed from one of her crippling headaches, which would go misdiagnosed for at least a decade as doctors tried to push Valium at her.

Splayed open on the examination table, my feet were trapped in unyielding stirrups and other regions invaded by icy instruments. The young ER doctor's blue latex-gloved hands and pale, color-match eyes offered little in the way of bedside manner. I shut my eyes tight, ashamed of my uncharacteristic waterfall of tears, but I was dying!

"Do you have sex with boys?" The doctor's voice cut clearly through the din in the room and the pounding pain that had by then spread to the crown of my head.

Boys? *BoySS*?? But I'm not one of *those* girls! Wouldn't this doctor be shocked to learn that I could identify him as a first-year resident? That I was friends with a program director at New York University Medical Center? That I was an A student, pre-med at a New England college?

But even if I wasn't, what did his tactless inquiry have to do with my period?

I had fallen in love my sophomore year, but my boyfriend agreed we would wait. Well, there was that one time... We did a bit of exploring... Oh, Lord, did something happen? Did I somehow cause this pain?!

"Do you have sex with boys?!" The question attacked me again and felt more invasive than the implement that probed my insides.

"YES!" I only had strength for a one-word answer, and that word seemed closer to the truth than its opposite. But I would have admitted to anything, withstood any abuse, just to earn some... relief.

Dr. Pale Eyes scoffed with a satisfied smirk as he notated my chart. As if he'd gathered sufficient anecdotal evidence to support some sort of thesis. I imagined him laughing with drunken Anglo buddies, exchanging ill-gotten data, and concocting some B.S. mythology about Black girls.

The exam was complete. My symptoms and I were dismissed, like a naughty school kid. Write on the white board of my mind 100 times: "I will press my legs tight together to prevent egress or ingress."

In real life, pick up the prescription-strength Tylenol and a heating pad. I was too sick and afraid to voice my concerns and questions. If Dr. Pale Eyes' interview really was designed to diagnose the cause of my agony, what now?

The scrip provided no help. But the shame of that night kept me away from a doctor for another twelve, tortuous months. I even had to run out ten minutes into Stevie Wonder's "Innervisions" concert because I could not hide my bleeding. Mortified, I picked a quarrel with my boyfriend as an excuse for leaving.

Finally, during my junior year, a nurse practitioner at the college infirmary educated me on the clinical term for my severe dysmenorrhea. She prescribed birth control pills, standard treatment for out-of-control periods.

I didn't tell my parents I was on the pill. I was too afraid Daddy might agree with Pale Eyes that I was one of those girls.

But wait a minute! *Whatever* kind of woman I am, or anyone thinks I am, shouldn't we all expect to have our medical symptoms taken seriously? Or is that only me?

#

In March 2022, a *New York Times* article is picked up by news outlets worldwide: "Women Are Calling Out 'Medical Gaslighting.' Studies show female patients and people of color are more likely to have their symptoms dismissed by medical providers."

So, no, Ashton, it wasn't only you.

What is "gaslighting"? The term comes from Gas Light, a 1938 play that was later a movie starring Ingrid Bergman and Charles Boyer. In the story, a husband slowly dupes his wife into questioning her reality and her sanity. He starts out by tampering with their gas lamps so they flicker on and off at times when only his wife can see. Medical gaslighting has become a popular term to describe healthcare professionals downplaying or dismissing patients' reported symptoms. There has been some pushback from the healthcare industry on the use of the term gaslighting. After all, unlike the faithless and manipulative husband in the movie, healthcare providers are not *deliberately* trying to make patients question their sanity, are they? Nevertheless, medical studies conducted in recent years have precipitated a rash of reports on the subject. Like the one reported in WebMD in January 2023: "Medical Gaslighting: When the Doctor Dismisses Your Concerns. Research has shown that women, people of color, older people, non-heterosexual people, and individuals with 'stigmatized' conditions—like being overweight or having a mental illness—are more frequently misdiagnosed and their symptoms are more frequently dismissed."

Back in college, I was at the intersection of the first two of those risk factors. Now, I present with four out of five so I must be extra diligent. When I prepare for a doctor visit, I write a list of my symptoms and questions, then make sure they are all addressed. If there were ever to come a time when I could not understand my doctor (say my hearing became bad or my mind fuzzy), I'd ask a smart friend to accompany me. If I feel a physician repeatedly brushes aside my concerns, I'll find another doctor. That happened to me about ten years ago, with a *female* gynecologist no less!

Those hellish monthly periods plagued me on and off for decades. Then in 2019, I was diagnosed with uterine fibroids and, since I was past childbearing age, my doctor advised we just "remove the organ." (From my own research, I learned that Black women are two to three times more likely than other races to have recurring fibroids or suffer from complications.) While I was very happy with my GYN at the time, I still sought out another opinion before having the surgery.

Recently, I was invited to perform a reading of *The 1619 Project: A New Origin Story*, the book created by Pulitzer Prize-winner Nikole Hannah-Jones as an expansion of the essays presented in *The New York Times Magazine*. My assigned passages were from the chapter on Medical Care, which echoed studies reported in the news. Preparing for this performance prompted my recall of that cursed episode in the emergency room. Once I made the connection, I knew I'd have to share my story. As Nina Simone said, "You can't help it. An artist's duty, as far as I'm concerned, is to reflect the times."

I feel sick recalling that winter of 1974, and other times, when the thought entered my mind that good credentials should make me more deserving of care than another person in my situation. I'm ashamed that—even for a moment—I imagined one of "those girls" would necessarily receive less respect.

As with many things in our lives, women must take responsibility for our own well-being. I'd love to be able to depend on the physicians with all their degrees and all their training. Just do what they prescribe and be done with it. But I am thankful for the experiences and knowledge that taught me I am my own best advocate—no longer vulnerable and helpless, but secure, steadfast, and powerful.

space program for niggas

an erasure poem(s) of Elon Musk's Mars & Beyond: the Road to Making Humanity Multiplanetary statement

by ASHUNDA NORRIS

from TAINT TAINT TAINT

*

wake up the future
be great— a spacefaring civilization
. be ing future thinking future
be more
go there and be stars.

*

You the morning the future go
be a civilization all
about
better And more
exciting out being stars.

*

want the future
be
the future think the future
I
go be among stars.

note: the title is an erasure of the A Tribe Called Quest song Ain't No Space Program for Niggas

Falling

By SABA WAHEED

from The Margins

Rami was riding ahead of her, his control over the bike unsteady. Naira watched his knees rise to the handlebars and realized she should have raised the seat. He was nervous and overthinking what he was doing. Trying to go slow when he should go fast.

"We can go up the hill just a little bit and then turn around," she said. This street was used to pick up students at the elementary school, but it was empty today since it was the weekend. The road was long, part-flat and part-hill. When Rami started to turn the bike, he reduced his speed too much so that the bike dropped to the side. He jumped off.

Naira caught up and circled around him, "You okay?"

"Yes," he said with a tinge of frustration.

She didn't get off her bike. She wanted him to learn to fall so that he would stop being afraid of it. His mother was one of her oldest friends, and Naira noticed how her friend was overly protective of Rami, similar to the way they'd been brought up. Rami's family had moved to this suburban part of LA, with homes that had high walls and security cameras. Naira could see tennis courts and swimming pools through the tiny slits in the wall-high shrubbery.

"Still want to go?" she asked.

Rami took a long moment before he finally uttered, "Okay."

Naira looked up the hill and saw a car turn onto the street. She moved to the sidewalk expecting it to pass by them. But the car stopped halfway down the road and pulled to the side.

"It's okay, we can go around it," she said to Rami.

They started again, and Naira rode alongside Rami as they passed the vehicle. It was a dark blue Honda Accord with a new-car shine to it. She glanced in and could see a man sitting in the driver seat. He was looking at something on his face in the rear-view mirror. When they got to the end of the street, she asked if Rami wanted to go again.

"Yes." His face was flushed, and he was slightly out of breath but he was already looking down the road with anticipation. When they passed the car again, the man was outside with a spray bottle and roll of paper. He was wiping away dried-up spots on his windshield.

"That's my teacher," Rami said after they passed him. "From third grade. Mr. Blinkin."

Naira waited for him to say more, but he didn't. She had to pedal harder as they reached the incline. She had been using an app for a daily home workout and could feel her body ready to endure. Halfway up the hill, they turned around. "Just stay to the left, and you won't have to worry about the car," Naira said.

They started down the hill and Naira pedaled faster. She felt the freeness of the wind blowing in her face, the rush of speed filling up her body. As she pushed forward, her bike sounded like an engine. Suddenly, the world had no burdens. Her friend, Rami's mother, wasn't home sick and bedridden. The whole world hadn't just experienced a year of grief and isolation.

Life was there, and it was to be lived and breathed-in fully.

She felt tears slide down her face.

She reached the end of the street and only then realized Rami wasn't next to her. She looked back up the street. The blue Honda was still parked, but the man was gone.

Her heart was pumping fast as she flew up the street. When she got to the car, she saw that the school gate next to it was open. She pulled her bike up to the curb and let it drop. On the school grounds, there were tents up for outdoor classes and a community garden with shriveled-up plants. The glare of the blacktop made it hard to see. She left the playground to head for the classrooms, where she found an open door. The classroom was as generic as any other—tables lined up, child-sized seats, amateur art on the walls. The teacher sat in the front of the class with his head down on the desk. Rami was next to him, his mask on.

The teacher looked up. His eyes were bloodshot. He was old, his hair completely white with a small balding spot. He was wearing a faded yellow button-down shirt and khaki pants.

"I saw him crying and followed him." Rami looked at her, his eyes wide and full. His black hair reached his shoulder, messy from a year of home cuts. He got up and stood next to the man. "His wife and daughter died. From COVID."

"I'm sorry," the teacher said, seeming to snap out of something, "You all shouldn't be here. I shouldn't have let him in."

"No, it's okay," Naira said. "Rami was your student.'

He turned to the boy. "You were?"

"It was a long time ago." Rami seemed so much older than his eleven years. "My mom is leaving too."

Naira felt her stomach tighten. He knew. He knew before any of them did. Before Naira could even admit those words to herself. Her oldest friend was leaving.

"Come on auntie, let's go to the top of the hill. You'll be okay, Mr. Blinkin." The teacher forced a smile as they walked outside. Naira turned back and saw him crumple again onto the table.

Rami cycled ahead of her, and both of them strained as the incline got steeper. They got to the top and Naira could hear the birds around her bantering. She looked up at the high walls. There were some things even they couldn't keep out.

She turned to Rami. "You want to talk about it...about your mom?"

Rami's gaze followed a butterfly that flew between them. He looked at Naira and then down the road. "No," he said finally. "I want to ride."

Rami pedaled hard ahead of her, going faster than before. And then she heard it—a deep, guttural, stormy scream. It was coming from Rami. She opened her mouth wide, and joined him.

Phenomenon of Fire

by NANCY LYNÉE WOO

from I'd Rather Be Lightning

to be small is to hear / sirens everywhere
waking / an emergency / counting / years in gasps
barking / dogs on a street corner / biting at nothing

to be unwell is to stay behind / a chain link fence
gripping / they can see you / through it
constant / swivel / quick pivot

to be poor and educated is to spin / like a top
on the dinner tables of America / naïve / with dreams
that everyone can be free / by looking at the stars

to be a woman is to be a balloon / drifting
a sway among clouds / body / out of a body / out of a body
danger / an empty room / full of barking dogs

to be small is a long cold spell / electrocuting a power / line
to be unwell is a deluge / a man raging /
to be poor and educated is thousands / of tiny collisions
to be a woman is to choose / how to be / either still or useful

I choose high voltage / kick-ass survival
an untangling / rapid motion
small sparks / catching

I'd rather be / jolting back / into my body
inhabiting / the ghost / of my former ghost
a coming-back-home / after years away
an everywhere kind of feeling / a big voice now

\ when I speak /
\ a line of fire blazes /
\ across the field /
\ poppies bloom /
\ all the way /
\ around /
\ the mountain /

Naysaying the Noise

by NANCY LYNÉE WOO

from West Trade Review

I haven't found one thing the stars
aren't a cure for. Hand me my mountain

bag, full of ripe plums plummeting
from flower bud to boiling pot to jam jar.

I count the miles back out to chaparral,
heaving under the weight of my need

to see everything, and to be seen seeing it.
Would I feel less wanderlust if I could

scrub off the dead glory of a nation
obsessed with itself? Follow me

to a hot spring tucked away
behind some tall grass—

would you like that? I accelerate
out to the wilderness, forgetting

what I'm supposed to be forgetting.
To get absolutely lost in the ridiculous

brilliance of an acorn—I have everything
I could ever want. And still I wonder

how far humanity will go for a profit,
whether we will ever find another home

like this one, its miraculous blue, its hilarious
oxygen. Every cat meme is a metaphor

for the existential threat *du jour*. Somewhere,
a teenage girl thinks her ears are too big.

And the hawking jays, what I wouldn't even call
song. I want to give them to you, their pointy heads

and blue breasts flashing. What illusion am I breaking
when I say no to the noise? I won't entertain hatred,

refuse to listen to vitriolic propaganda no black bear,
no bobcat, no oriole, no waxing moon understands.

Revolutionary

by MONONA WALI

The pistol sits in my palm, cold, black, mocking. Maria has put it there. I'm lying in a hammock in her home in Arcatao, El Salvador. It's December 1988, and the country is in its ninth year of a brutal civil war.

"Monona, *guerrillera,*" she says to me. "*Revolucionaria.*" It's her pistol. The one she carries in a holster strapped to her waist. She has taken my hand and placed it in my palm; a taunt and an invitation to join the revolution.

I know the import of the gesture; I know she is offering me a fork in the road.

I take the pistol and tuck it into the front of my pants. I'm smiling, but even now, thirty-five years later, I remember the answer clearly in my head.

How does one become a revolutionary, someone who takes up arms, who risks one's life, to bring down the government? It is vital to get the answers to fulfill the mission of the documentary film which we, co-director Pamela Cohen, cinematographer John Knoop, and I are making to put a human face on the civil war, a war that has ravaged the country, and left 70,000 dead, mostly civilians. The subject of the film is Maria, Maria Ofelia Navarette de Dubon, a thirty-eight-year-old mother of three who has become a leader in the FMLN, the Farabundo Marti National Liberation Front. It will be called *Maria's Story.*

Arcatao is a small pueblo on the Honduran border in the very northern end of Chalatenango province and it is here, in Maria's hometown, that we hope to get some answers to the question. Pam, John and I are American citizens, and our government is giving aid to the Salvadoran government to the tune of 1.5 million dollars a day. The conflict has been painted as a cold war era fight against the communist influence of Cuba and Russia in Central America. We are here to expose the absolute lie of this policy and we are going to do it by telling the story of Maria, her family, and the journey of her life from campesina to armed revolutionary. To make the film, we are pioneering a new consumer video camera just put out by Sony. We plan to transfer the footage to 16mm once we return to the US. This will enable us to give the film a theatrical release. John Knoop has adapted a simple solar power charging system for the batteries that run the cameras. Without this new technology, it would not have been possible to make the film. We had learned the hard way—several months earlier we had arrived in Chalatenango fully equipped with 16mm camera, Nagra sound recorder, and reels of film. We had not counted on a military offensive in the area that lasted over a month, and that kept Maria on the run. Weighed down with all our gear, we would have been a risk to her and to the guerrillas, not to mention ourselves. We had regrouped, and this time all our gear fits into our backpacks.

If anyone can tell the story of the civil war that can grab the hearts and minds of the American public, it is Maria. She is like a small round Yoda, her broad face framed by short hair (we had filmed a scene where José, her husband, gives her a haircut), her stocky body clothed in a tee shirt and a simple blue cotton skirt. Her feet are clad in black boots that are worn and coming unstitched. Arcatao is central to Maria's life story, but because of army presence in this area, the road, accessible only by foot, has been off-limits until now. We are excited to be here and be able to film her in the home she and José lived in before the war came violently to their doorstep nine years earlier, forcing them to flee into the mountains and survive on roots and berries.

We are gathered in their outdoor kitchen—chickens are roaming about, a tall mango tree provides a shady canopy for the brick-laid courtyard, and smoke rises in a thin trail from the small wood fireplace. By now we have spent almost two months with Maria, the camera trained on her at all times as she moves between guerrilla encampments hidden in verdant mountains not unlike the Southern California hills where Pam and I hiked to get in shape for the film. Maria plans war strategy with other guerrilleros, but her main role is to rally the civilian population to join in the resistance.

Over the next few days in Arcatao, we film Maria walking the rough cobblestone streets, walking through the school where she had only been able to study until fourth grade, before being forced to work as a maid to help her mother and nine siblings survive. She loved studying—and even at thirty-eight, it is still her dream to return to school, to get her college education. Before agreeing to marry José, she made him promise that he would allow her to go back to school.

She takes us into a building next door to their home, now an empty shell of a building, eerily quiet and strewn with broken bricks, that had been converted to a National Guard headquarters while she was still living next door. She tells us the story of hearing the screams of people being tortured, no doubt people she knew. She's spooked being in there and hurries out. We're spooked too.

Later, she and José snuggle into a hammock together. José is small and muscular, a man whose body has been toughened by hard work, who looks like a cowboy, not in the romantic John Wayne mold, but the real thing, with broken teeth and gnarled hands. He also works for the FMLN as a supplier of food and other goods. Because of their work, they are often separated, and their reunions are grand occasions. This is one of them, and to see them both together is very moving.

Together they tell the story of the day the military came rolling into the town with tanks and trucks to round up young men not already conscripted into the army, and union organizers of which Maria had been one, organizing coffee plantation workers for better wages, health care and education. They stayed trapped in their home and started to sing so as not to let on their fear. It was shortly after that they fled into the surrounding hills with their young daughters. The writing was on the wall. If they stayed, they would have been killed. It was in the hills that Maria began to organize other peasants who also faced near starvation and only had each other to rely on. They started to encounter FMLN soldiers, young men and women who had taken up arms against the government. She was always clear about what she was fighting for—food, healthcare, and education—basic humane living conditions, none of which she had experienced growing up. It was in the hills that she decided to join the FMLN and take up arms. By then she had seen enough of what her government had done to its people.

On the way to Arcatao, we had stopped at a high bank looking down on the Rio Sumpul. The bridge over the river had been bombed and had only recently been boarded over with planks allowing foot crossing. We filmed Maria as she recounted the story of the massacres that the Salvadoran army had perpetrated in 1980, 1982 and 1984. "This river is a mute witness of so much pain of our people," she said. "Hundreds of bodies have passed by here." Her face tightened in anger and anguish, the two emotions that seem to fuel her. The story of the massacres at the river had become one of the legendary atrocities of the war, but that went unreported in the American media.

And there were many more stories. One day as we filmed, Maria and José told the story of how their own daughter, Ceci, the eldest of three, had been killed in an army ambush. She was just nineteen. She joined the FMLN when she was fourteen. Maria said, "I've never felt so much hatred for the enemy. Not so much because they killed her because we are making war, them against us, and us against them. But after they killed her, they stripped her and mutilated her. They slit her from bottom to top. It was horrible. the anger I felt. It revives my rage!"

We had seen many young children carrying rifles in the FMLN. We knew this would be a point of controversy for American audiences. We confronted Maria. How could this be justified? Her answer had been very clear. "If you adopt the armed struggle, it's not because it's the most wonderful thing in the world. It's that love of life is instinctive. Even animals have it. When you see the possibility of saving your life, you save it. And if that means picking up a gun you pick it up." That, in short, was her reason for taking up arms against the government, for becoming a revolutionary.

Ironically, it was this answer that helped me define my own answer to her invitation to join the revolution. Looking back on that scene, the gun neatly tucked in my pants, I see myself, thirty-three years old, my long black hair in a braid, wearing khaki pants, and my feet clad in very broken-in and beloved lace-up boots. I was so thin from a diet of tortillas and beans that I had stopped menstruating. Making *Maria's Story* had been the grand adventure of my life. The project had drawn me the moment Pam approached me about co-directing with her. We had come to the project very differently. She had instigated it out of her work as a Central American activist. Like me, she was from a liberal east coast upbringing—in her case Jewish, in mine, Indian immigrant, daughter of two academics who believed deeply in the words "with liberty and justice for all." I had recently completed an MFA in filmmaking from UCLA Film School and Pam brought me on board the documentary to help craft a compelling dramatic story. By that time, Pam had already gotten approval from the FMLN and was actively working on fundraising. She had met Maria on one of her early forays in El Salvador and brilliantly recognized that Maria would be the perfect subject to put a human face on the war. Every pore of her skin exuded warmth and humanity. She did not have an insincere bone in her body. Who she was on camera was who she was in real life. Yes, she could be a performer, but there was no disconnect between her revolutionary vision and the very essence of her being.

When Maria handed me the gun, I knew I would not join the revolution. Was I just too bourgeois in my upbringing to imagine myself holstering a gun? Was it a deep antipathy to gun culture that I associated with conservatism and Western colonialism? Was it the husband I had waiting at home? The parents I didn't dare break the hearts of? The children I knew I wanted to bear? I am sure they were already suffering enough knowing I was here. Yes, all those things. But something else too. Some resistance in me that was the voice of a skeptic. Did I want to die for this cause? Was there any cause I was willing to die for?

A few days before arriving in Arcatao, we had been following Maria and some of the FMLN soldiers from one village to another. One of the soldiers got word on his radio that there was a battalion of soldiers in the area. Maria urged us to move quickly. We were in a large open area of tall dry grass with no cover. We began running. We could hear a helicopter hovering nearby. My heart began to race. I remember thinking that if I was shot and bled to death in this field that it would be a pointless death. It was that moment that the reality of war hit me. War is a count of bodies. And those dead bodies seemed to count for nothing. Would there be a story about three journalists dying in El Salvador? Would it change the course of the war? Unlikely. After all, four American nuns had been murdered, not to mention Archbishop Oscar Romero. Those murders, well-publicized, had not altered the course of the war, although they had sparked an international solidarity movement. My death, Pam's death, John's death—none of us mattered enough. The reality of dying at thirty-three hit me. I would be a corpse on the ground, and that was it, mourned only by my family, my husband, and my close circle of friends.

I understood clearly the difference between myself and someone like Maria. She had no choice. I did. Although Pam, John and I decided to put ourselves in harm's way, our stay was on a limited meter of three months.

The choice I made, to be behind the camera, was enacting an identity for myself. As we filmed Maria telling the story of the massacres on the Rio Sumpul, as we filmed her and José recounting the story of the murder of their daughter, and as we filmed a moonlit family reunion, I had felt the thrill of knowing we were getting good footage for the film. There was always a part of my mind that belonged to the film, and not to the cause. But I think I saw the unwillingness to adopt a cause as a failure of sorts. If I could never be wholly invested in a position, who was I? In the time before identity politics became a thing, I was struggling to figure out what was the most authentic identity for myself. Even before the question of appropriation had become part of the national cultural conversation, I sensed that I should not be appropriating the cause of others. I was still searching for an identity, a voice. My first documentary had been about the Onondaga Nation's struggle for sovereignty. My UCLA thesis film *Grey Area* was a dramatic short about a young black television reporter who fights to use her voice to tell the true story of why black kids end up in jail. Both were honest and successful films, nevertheless, I sensed I should be telling stories closer to my own experience, that of an Indian immigrant, but that story had no legitimacy in my mind.

I think Maria knew that I would never pick up a gun and join the revolution. She also knew that the film had more power to bring about the change she desired than adding one more revolutionary soldier to the ranks. She fully embraced the mission of the film, although she had put herself reluctantly at its center.

The film aired on PBS in 1990 to an audience of over two million viewers. Maria and her story did indeed win the hearts and minds of the American public. The film started the desired national conversation on US funding of the Salvadoran government and military. Senator John McCain decried the film as propaganda on the US Senate floor, using it as an argument to cut funding to the Corporation of Public Broadcasting. But US Representative Ron Dellums said it should be required viewing for every member of Congress. The war was finally defunded in 1992, and the FMLN and the Salvadoran government signed a peace accord. The civil war ended.

The experience was transformative. It had to be. I was beginning to see that bringing about change, even more so revolutionary change, was a nuanced and complicated task. It could not be measured in years or even decades. At the end of the war, Maria followed her dream to return to school and to keep working for the betterment of her people. She left the FMLN, disgusted with the infighting and lack of meaningful action. In 2019, she was appointed the Minister of Local Development for the controversial government of Nayib Bukele, trying to get bridges and schools built. She remains an inspiration.

How to find my path, I realized, was going to be a constant work in progress. I became pregnant soon after returning from El Salvador and spent the nine months of gestation editing the film. My water broke the day we locked picture. The two joys will forever be linked. I had tentatively started writing fiction before making *Maria's Story*, but the commitment became absolute after we brought the film out in the world. Fiction offered a new door to understanding reality and the human experience, and another way to fight. Sometimes fiction offers me a feeling of unity—activist and writer—sometimes it splits me in two. It's ongoing, finding the balance, figuring out how to hold a gun, but never to use it.

Xochimilco Bakery, No. 3

By ROBERTA H. MARTÍNEZ

CHARACTERS

ROSANNA, Latina, early 30s, in mis-matched clothes that could be used for running or cleaning the house

YVETTE, Latina, early 30s, in well-coordinated athletic clothes and a fanny pack.

OFFICER DON CLARK, White, early 50s, INS uniform extremely neat, but well-worn.

OFFICER FILEMON "PHIL" ORTIZ, Latino, early 30s, INS uniform new and impeccably clean.

PANADERIA WORKERS; varying in age, from México and Central American countries.

TIME

April 20, 1997, Spring, early morning, weather is cool

PLACE

Small panaderia, TV with poor reception on shelf; sound fades in and out on U.S./Mexico soccer (FINAL 2-2).

Lights RISE.

YVETTE and ROSANNA finish run, chat outside panaderia

YVETTE

That was like a flashback from high school.

ROSANNA

Running track, dinner at my folk's place, watching TV.

YVETTE

Square Pegs, Dallas ... Fame.

ROSANNA

Dancing to Queen or Linda Ronstadt.

YVETTE

Your mom telling us to "lower the music."

ROSANNA

Memories.

YVETTE

Talk about memories. Haven't been in a panaderia in maybe 15 years. Wouldn't be here if I hadn't bumped into you at reunion!

ROSANNA

I couldn't stay away that long. Coming here ... coming home. *(Inhales deeply, taking in all of room).* Sweet bits of cultura—chilindrinas, niños envueltos ...

YVETTE

Marranitos, campechanas ...

ROSANNA AND YVETTE

Conchas!

ROSANNA

Jinx. *(They laugh).* It's good being back home, I come here and do some people watching as I drink my café de olla.

YVETTE

Thought you were kidding when you said you moved back. I've been thinking of buying ... but, not here. I like where I am; I know where the Starbuck's and the Panera is. I'm not home much anyway.

ROSANNA looks questioningly at YVETTE, who doesn't notice

YVETTE (CONT'D)

Your family always lived here, right?

ROSANNA

No, we started out in the Central Valley. Piscando…

YVETTE

Piscando?

ROSANNA

Picking—mostly fruit; moved around a lot. Grownups said the grapes had deeper roots than we did.

YVETTE

But when we were in school didn't your dad work at Sears?

ROSANNA

Yes, but first, he and a primo saved money so they could leave the field and come here. Then they brought us.

Cheers on TV. YVETTE points to TV

YVETTE

Who's playing?

ROSANNA

Dunno. If someone from El Centro was here, they'd know.

YVETTE

The place your mom started, right?

ROSANNA

She and some other organizers. El Centro de Acción en la Comunidad. *(Reflecting)* When we first moved here, we mostly heard Spanish, in high school mostly English.

YVETTE

And now back to Spanish. How'd you end up back here?

ROSANNA

When Eric and I married, we bought a house out in Rancho Cucamonga—good price, big house. I missed all of this *(Uses tongs to point to room).* I'd get homesick for the smell of tacos... frying in grasa. Eric never got that.

YVETTE

(Deadpan) Tacos. The reason you left a big house in Rancho.

ROSANNA

Kind of... Eric and me—not a good match. Rancho neighbors and me—no match. The bigger the house, the better your life. Commuting hours and hours a day to a house you don't have time to enjoy. I hated it.

YVETTE

I wouldn't move back here. No point. *(Shrugs)* Parents gone; all my sibs Orange County. Besides, I'm looking to "where I'm going" not "where I've been".

ROSANNA

Hmm. After my mom's stroke, I came back to help her. Before I knew it, she had me covering a lot of her hours at El Centro. Turns out I'm good at helping folks figure out how to stand up for themselves.

Good play—cheers

YVETTE

I guess. *(Looks at tongs and laughs, redirects)* Remember Junior year? "Relay all the way"

YVETTE reaches for tongs from ROSANNA who misses a beat and then joins in the motion

And how many times did we place?

ROSANNA AND YVETTE

Every time!!

They high five

YVETTE

Remember when Mrs. Johnson had you run laps and you wouldn't, because you "hadn't been talking"?

ROSANNA

Well, I hadn't.

YVETTE

It wasn't a big deal.

ROSANNA

It was to me. I hadn't talked. I didn't do anything wrong.

YVETTE

It bugged me that you didn't apologize.

ROSANNA

But I did—eventually. I knew she'd keep the rest of you running laps until I apologized. What a power trip. She shouldn't have done that to you.

YVETTE

But she did. Nothing we could do about it.

Uncomfortable BEAT; YVETTE tries to lighten mood, placating tone

You're right about the people watching here. That couple there look like they're buying enough for a party. Maybe First Communion?

ROSANNA

"Pasteles para toda ocasión."

YVETTE

Do you talk to any of them?

ROSANNA

Not the other customers, but one day, I can't help myself. I ask Sarita, behind the counter, "Where are Xochimilco Bakery, Number 1 and Xochimilco Bakery, Number 2?" She says, "En Montebello". *(Spanish pronunciation).*

YVETTE

How did you not laugh out loud? Back in the day there wouldn't have been any panaderia in Monteh-bel-lo. Still wouldn't be one in most cities with a Hilton.

Chant on TV—USA, USA

ROSANNA

The hotel chain. You said you travel a lot for your job?

YVETTE

(Glancing up at TV, nods in affirmation)

Always ready to hit the road for Hilton. Last week, last-minute flight to Canada. Montreal. Quebec City—like being in Europe... but without the red tape. Fanny pack and passport always ready... so many places to see. Up the corporate ladder... management here I come. (Beat) You travel much?

ROSANNA

Nah, always been more of a home body. Especially now. Besides, plenty to see here. Lots of characters here.

YVETTE

Right, like the neighbor with the barky Chihuahua.

ROSANNA

Sra. Gomez and Chulita. Chulita, la Chihuahua. Both of them... always into everyone else's business. They're funny—when they get excited, they sort of sound the same. (Imitates yappy/ chisme sounds). I shouldn't talk, sometimes I make up stories for the gente here.

YVETTE

Like…

ROSANNA

That fellow over there, he's… a jornalero.

YVETTE

A what?

ROSANNA

Day laborer. The men that stand on the corner; for someone to drive up and hire them for the day. He came here in '95. Likes atole and the pan dulce shaped like elotes.

Continue in a silent animated conversation

Stage right, CLARK and ORTIZ outside panaderia

OFFICER ORTIZ

Don, I thought we were going to the Garment District.

OFFICER CLARK

We'll get to the maquiladoras, every rookie knows them. But I know places most agents don't think of. The element of surprise, you know. Watching them scatter…

OFFICER ORTIZ

But this is a panaderia. They're just going to buy some bread and go home.

OFFICE CLARK

Can't be too sure of that now, can we? Who knows what they might be planning. Look at them, old, young, pregnant—lot of variety in this store. Happy hunting.

Clark and then Ortiz enter and hold up badges. Tongs, trays drop; gasps and hushed tones.

This is a raid! Everyone stay where you are! Don't try to run, we have vans and agents waiting outside.

OFFICER ORTIZ

(Struggles with Spanish)

Esta es una incur-sión. No traten de correr. Tenemos los…los vans a-fue-ra.

ROSANNA

La Migra.

YVETTE

What?

ROSANNA

INS raid. Damn. They're going to take in gente without papers.

YVETTE

Why? They're not doing anything wrong. They're not breaking any laws. They're just buying pan dulce.

PANADERIA WORKERS

OS accents, regional and national dialects—concern and fear

Including: Qué va a pasar con mi hija?

Yvette and Rosanna watch in disbelief

OFFICER CLARK

(Enjoys questioning Yvette in mocking tone.)

Green card.

YVETTE

What?

CLARK glares at YVETTE; ROSIE weighs exchange

OFFICER CLARK

Papeles. Grin card.

YVETTE

I have this.

YVETTE hands over passport

OFFICER CLARK

Hand it over.

(Barely glances at it, then Hands it back)

That'll do.

(To ROSANNA, who reaches for pockets not there)

Pasaporte.

(Voices grow louder from back of bakery)

ROSANNA

I'm sorry, sir, but I can call my mother and ask her to have someone bring my passport.

OFFICER CLARK

Green Card?

(Walking closer to ROSANNA. Both become more formal in stance.)

Announcer softly, "Goal"

ROSANNA

(Surprised and affronted; answers in confrontational tone.)

Crowd on TV cheers.

Excuse me.

OFFICER CLARK

I said, where's your Green Card or your birth certificate.

ROSANNA

When I woke up this morning, I didn't think I'd need to prove my citizenship. Here's my driver's license.

(Angrily, offers driver's license); Clark distracted by someone leaving, shouts to Ortiz

CLARK

Ortiz! (Or-tis)

YVETTE (TO ROSIE)

What are you doing? Calm down. We'll be okay.

ROSANNA

(Growing more frustrated with Yvette)

What do you mean?

YVETTE

We're not like them. It's not our problem.

ROSANNA

It is my problem. It's yours, too. They're our gente. Who do you think you are? How can you just watch?

CLARK

(Returns focus to ROSANNA who has her driver's license)

You.

ROSANNA

My driver's license.

OFFICER CLARK

Come on, Mamita.

ROSANNA

Dr. Rosanna Rodriguez.

OFFICER CLARK

(Takes license without looking at it, looks straight at her)

What color are your eyes?

YVETTE

(Almost whispering to herself)

Tell him. Say it, Rosie. He's not Mrs. Johnson!

ROSANNA

What color do they look like to you?

CLARK and ROSANNA stare at each other

OFFICER CLARK

I can't tell.

CLARK and ROSANNA continue stare. YVETTE responds in disbelief

Looks like we'll be taking a ride together.

(Announces to all, fine pronunciation)

Mujeres—una linea, hombres—otra.

OFFICER ORTIZ

One got away.

OFFICER CLARK

No sweat, Ortiz, we have another one here.

CLARK exits. ROSANNA looks to YVETTE. ORTIZ walks behind, looking towards door

YVETTE

What are you doing?

ROSANNA

I've got to go with them. I'll know what to do from inside. Call my mom. She'll be able to help from outside.

Yvette shakes head in disbelief

ROSANNA

Please. Call her. We need your help.

End of game cheers

ORTIZ and ROSANNA exit

YVETTE bewildered, alone on stage, almost stumbles on tray and tongs

YVETTE

(In anger, frustration, and fear)

Now what?

(Picks up tongs and tray at her feet. Considers, looking toward Rosanna, then audience)

Now what?

CURTAIN

Self Portrait, With and Without

after Chen Chen

by SHELLY HOLDER

With a headache. With an extra-large water I might or might not finish off,
despite the “knowledge” it’s the “best” cure for whatever thing ailing me.
Without knowing the number of prayers said for me or if they worked. With
dog hair but no dog. With bleeding cuticles and bug bites I worry into scars.
With my father’s watchful eye to catch my aimless, anxious hands, his quick
“Don’t pick!” when one strays too close to a wound. Without -cures, mani- or pedi-,
because I am ashamed of what I have mangled. With a love for rain, falling water,
because of this desert-raised body, always thirsting for something I cannot name.
With a name that means a grassy cliff, and me, barren of meadows With
barrenness and premature menopause. With cataracts. With pain. Without cancer.
Without the chemo curls I loved, but with growing determination for a perm.
With no particular love for the ‘80s, or neon colors, or pop culture. With problematic love

for leggings as pants, given the Germanic hips and rear end. With nature documentaries
playing in the background. With Audible playing me to sleep. With waking up tired,
no matter how many hours I get. With bugs I call features without conviction.
With a phobia of moths. With all the spiders I catch-and-release outside, squealing
the whole time. With phone calls that consist of more squealing, "I did it, I dealt
with the spider all by myself!" because Mom can't come kill them for me anymore.
With fear of my father's mother's dementia. With fear of my mother's father's dementia.
Without guarantee of making it to old age, graceful or otherwise. With Dad's stories
about his father, outliving the doctor who gave him a year, and how it became
a catchphrase against smalltown pity: "Well, show me your guarantee." How Grandpa died
of cancer regardless. With all the stats charting how "cured" is the equivalent of
"next time, I'll get a different kind." With so many "oughts" they drain me of water,
that building block of flourish, or maybe they drown me, I'm always without certainty.
With the way I wash away the world: with poetry, with poetry. With poetry.

You Know What They Say About a Body in Motion

by SHELLY HOLDER

And so I repeat it to the couch, my thighs.
I repeat it within the always moving elevator,
metal walls bouncing half syllables back
instead of finding the stairway's restful places.
What they say now has been a truth forever,
and I whisper it into the once-in-a-while storm,
over the leaves of the orange tree that does not
bear fruit. As for the grinding fan, flickering
internet, slow heat, I remind us all just a hint
of momentum will carry us into that state
where we cannot stop.

A Room of (Almost) My Own

by LIZ GONZÁLEZ

from Poets & Writers Magazine

When I was single, I never needed a room of my own. I wrote whenever I wanted, day or night, in my tiny studio apartment where I lived alone. Drafts of poems and stories and books would be strewn about for days, undisturbed. My clerical job didn't require me to take work home; I could even write at my desk when business was slow.

My unencumbered writing life changed considerably twenty years ago when I earned a graduate degree and fell in love in the same year. After graduation, my boyfriend—now husband—Jorge and I moved into an apartment together. I soon joined the ranks of adjunct instructors commuting across congested Southern California freeways to teach at community colleges and universities.

My writing suffered.

I used the dinette as an office and stole two or three hours a week to write on our small dining table, when it wasn't being used for eating, lesson planning, grading papers, paying bills, or other activities. I had difficulty switching from my hectic life into writer mode. My creativity needed to be eased into gear, and I couldn't escape reminders of the tasks waiting for me to complete—grading, cleaning, and more. I longed for a room of my own where I could shut the door and immerse myself in the world of the piece I was writing. I wanted a room I could decorate to express my eclectic taste and inspire me.

Ten years ago Jorge and I became first-time homeowners. Finally I had a room of my own—almost. We lived in Long Beach, California, where home prices were rising. All we could afford was an old 765-square-foot house with two bedrooms and one bathroom in a working-class neighborhood. The guest room, its size more suitable for a child, doubled as my writing and schoolwork room. To make it welcoming for overnight guests, I decorated it in neutral blue and brown hues, not the bright aqua, hot pink, Prince purple, and poppy orange I prefer. I did not display many of my cherished decorations. My doll collection, images and sculptures of Our Lady of Guadalupe, and ofrendas for dead loved ones might seem odd, tacky, or even frightening to guests. Although I couldn't fully express myself in the décor and had to frequently relinquish the space for visitors, I relished having a separate place to write.

A scientist by day and musician by night, Jorge turned the bonus room behind our detached garage into his music room and bedroom. I'm a night owl, and he wakes up at 4:30 in the morning to get ready for work, so we've slept in separate bedrooms since we first moved in together. He sealed and painted the bonus room, laid laminate wood flooring over the concrete, and installed bars on the windows and a security screen door.

Within a few months the local newspaper ran articles about recent break-ins in the neighborhood, and I felt unsafe sleeping in the house alone. Jorge was happy to move into the guest room—my writing room. He had grown weary of walking across the backyard to the house to shower on chilly winter mornings.

We decided to share the now-vacant bonus room. Jorge rented a small storage unit for the music equipment he used infrequently. We hung long curtains from the ceiling to divide our spaces. One side was his rehearsal space; the other was my office. Because of our different schedules, we each had the room to ourselves: I used it during the day before teaching night classes and Jorge at night after work.

This arrangement didn't last long. Jorge has many good qualities, but neatness isn't one of them. Whenever he prepared for an upcoming music performance, it looked like the Santa Ana winds had blown through the room. He left electric cords and gadgets scattered on the floor, my desk, and every other surface. His mess often remained there for up to a week, until he had time to put things away. I soon gave him back the bonus room. We needed the money he spent on the storage unit anyway. I stored my office furniture in the bonus room and garage and moved my writing materials into my bedroom.

The living room became my work space, where I used a laptop cart that I rolled into my bedroom when I finished writing for the day. Again I had difficulty switching into writer mode. This time I didn't have a table on which to handwrite ideas and early drafts, nowhere to set the materials that were integral to my writing process—multicolored pens, a writing journal, and literature and images that inspired me. My creativity stifled, I focused on writing short poems and accepted that they would evolve slowly.

Working in the living room sufficed until three years ago when I began developing two historical creative nonfiction book projects: one about my maternal grandmother's experiences growing up as a Mexican American in San Bernardino, California, and the other about my maternal grandfather's experiences growing up in the Midwest as a Mexican immigrant—both in the early 1900s. These were the most challenging writing endeavors I'd undertaken. The works had to honor my grandparents and do justice to the underheard Mexican and Mexican American history in their stories. To be as productive as possible, I *needed* a space where I could drop into the world of the draft I was working on, have my research and writing materials handy, and work without interruption. I tried to make a writing space work in every possible room. The kitchen nook was tight and drafty. My desk fit in my bedroom but not with my chair. I turned one-third of the already cramped living room into a writing space and worked there for a few months. The drawback was that I had to tidy my desk whenever guests came over, and I had to stop working when Jorge watched TV. I returned to working on the laptop cart in the living room, moving it and my materials to the bedroom at the end of my writing sessions.

By June 2019, I had grown frustrated and despondent because I had made little progress on my book projects. I was turning sixty in August and felt my mortality catching up with me. My father had died in an accident a few days after his twenty-fourth birthday when I was three; I know how uncertain life is. Finishing my two book projects before I died became a priority.

The only solution was to move back into the bonus room. I knew Jorge wouldn't mind. He has always been supportive of my writing. He also hadn't been able to rehearse in the room for over a year because his equipment and boxes were crammed into it. I called it the abyss.

I presented him with a plan for how to rearrange his stuff. He would continue rehearsing in his bedroom. We would hang the divider curtains in the bonus room again and store his temperature-sensitive equipment behind it. And we would hire a handyworker to seal the garage so he could store his other things in there. He agreed and promised to be mindful of not leaving his belongings in my part of the room.

Eager to start working in the bonus room, I asked Jorge to free up a corner for me. While cleaning the window frames, I found termite debris. Thinking the frames required only spot treatments, I scheduled a termite inspection, moved in my desk, and set up my materials, including enlarged maps and images of the areas where my grandparents had lived. Having a space where my creative spirit could finally unfurl, I made more progress on my projects in one week working in that room than I had in three years. Jorge also accomplished a lot that week—moving his boxes to the patio, purging, and organizing.

Our work groove ended the day the termite inspector came. The bonus room and garage needed tent fumigation. We decided to get the garage sealed before getting the back structure tented, so we could move his things inside. Over the next week, I researched handyworkers, made calls, and interviewed them. We hired a guy with rave reviews on Yelp and Facebook. He didn't have an opening for three weeks, but we thought he was worth the wait. During this time, Jorge's schedule got busy, and he left his things spread out on the patio and in the bonus room. His messes looked like the piles of junk people dumped in open lots. I could no longer work at my desk and found myself back at the laptop cart in the living room.

To distract myself from my disappointment and to get ideas for how to arrange and decorate my room, I streamed videos of authors and poets giving tours of their writing rooms. A series that featured prominent British authors appealed to me most. Novelist Wendy Holden refurbished a garden shed the size of a backyard cottage. She decorated her "writing hut" with a record player, frilly lamps, and a chaise lounge. Her desk sat beneath a window that overlooked a verdant valley and rolling hills. Author Lady Antonia Fraser's "aerie" was on the fourth floor of her home. She had it renovated to resemble an Edwardian country bedroom. She could sit at her desk and look out the window into the treetops or relax on her rose-patterned couch that matched the wallpaper and read a book she pulled from her floor-to-ceiling bookshelves. It struck me that if best-selling authors needed a personalized sacred space to create, a struggling writer like me could benefit from one too. My passion to have a room of my own was intensified.

The morning the handyworker was scheduled to come finally arrived. We woke up early to clear out the garage. An hour after his scheduled arrival time, the handyworker at last replied to Jorge's multiple texts and voicemail messages asking where he was. He said he had a bad case of the flu and had to postpone the job. We gave him the benefit of the doubt and rescheduled for the following week.

I could handle waiting another week. But when he was a no-show again, I began a search for a new handyworker.

The setbacks got to me. I took them as signs that I didn't deserve to have a writing room because I wasn't financially contributing much to the household. I made only a meager income from my writing, and most of it was from giving readings, not from publishing. Shortly after I began working on my book projects, I resigned from my adjunct teaching position at the local community college due to debilitating chronic migraines. Almost every day I experienced a severe headache or migraine that left me drained and my head full of fuzz. Our finances took a hit. So did my ego. For most of my adult life, I had been self-supporting, which was a source of pride for me. I was raised by a self-sufficient single mother of four daughters and valued my financial independence.

Meanwhile, Jorge started making extra money by running sound for events. He assured me that he accepted the jobs because he enjoyed the work, not because he was concerned about our finances. I took his side jobs as more evidence that I didn't deserve space, especially since he, the breadwinner, had to give up a room of his own so I could have one.

I told Jorge I wanted to return to our original arrangement: He would keep the bonus room, and I would use the cart in the living room. He wouldn't have it. He insisted we keep going and continued moving his equipment onto the shelves he had arranged in the garage. I moved forward, but my enthusiasm was gone. We interviewed a few more handyworkers and hired another stranger. This handyworker signed a contract and fulfilled his commitment with no problems. Next, the garage and bonus room were tented for three days. The first week of August, two months after we began the process and three weeks before my sixtieth birthday, our move was complete.

I posted a call on Facebook for free or cheap tall cabinets to store my research materials. Michael, a friend and Chicano elder in the arts community whom I revere, offered me his deceased mother's custom-built hutch. For free! The shelves had sliding glass doors that would protect my antique research books and deep cabinets for my archives. Jose, a neighbor and local visual artist, borrowed his brother's truck and helped Jorge and me pick up the hutch and carry it into my writing room. My room was coming together better than I had imagined. Jorge's, Jose's, and Michael's generous support of my writing emboldened me to treat myself with the same care.

In the following weeks I organized my books and writing materials and unpacked and displayed my curiositos. Jorge helped me with my final task: hanging images on the walls. When I stepped into my writing room the next morning, a sense of gratitude overwhelmed me. For the first time I had a writing space of my own. It was filled with gifts from friends and family members who have supported my writing over the years: a print of a painting inspired by my first poem; an artistic broadside with an excerpt from another of my poems; the hutch that kept my research materials safe; images of Our Lady of Guadalupe; curiositos, such as the pen with a holder that Jorge brought back for me from his music tour in Japan and gave to me on our first date; and my grandfather's desk, where he wrote his memoir about growing up as a Mexican immigrant in the Midwest.

I treasured these gifts and never questioned whether I deserved them or not. They inspired me and reminded me that I had loved ones who believed in me and supported me without judgement or expectations. Today, they remind me to value myself and my writing.

Now I'm all about putting my nalgas in the chair. I've been taking a new medication that has decreased the number of days I'm in too much pain to work. I get as much accomplished on my projects as possible on those pain-free days. My self-doubt still gets to me now and then, and I curb it by writing.

Jorge has been mindful of giving me advance notice when he needs to get his equipment out of the room, and he rarely leaves things around. Through this experience, I've grown to understand that it's an honor to share the room with a person as generous, thoughtful, and talented as Jorge. I hope some of his good energy rubs off on me.

I don't have a view of a verdant valley or of treetops in a posh neighborhood, but my view enthralls me nonetheless. The window above my desktop frames the garden we've created over the years: fuchsia bougainvillea that monarch and painted lady butterflies alight upon, a nopal bursting with prickly pears and paddles that nourish me, a purple Mexican sage bush that bees and hummingbirds feast upon, and a fragrant, bountiful Meyer lemon tree that gives us fruit throughout the year. Overhead, hummingbirds, finches, and black phoebes perch on the power lines one at a time and chirp. I couldn't afford to paint the walls Prince purple or change the boring blue and brown hues of the throw pillows and sleeper sofa cover, but I gifted myself with inexpensive aqua cotton gauze curtains that greet me whenever I enter the room. Before I sit to write, I draw back those curtains and breathe in the view of my backyard paradise.

My room of almost my own is not nearly as tony as those of the wealthy authors. My furniture is beat up and mismatched. My décor is a hodgepodge of different styles, themes, and cultures. Some of my curiositos are cheap, chipped, crooked, or glued back together. Nothing is of significant monetary value. Yet this room is invaluable to me—a place where I can read, think, research, stare out the window, meditate, do yoga, journal, make crafts, dance, and, most of all, write.

I've Already Been

By LISBETH COIMAN

the orchid pollinated by deceit
the honest hibiscus   hiding her own beauty at nights
the wild passion fruit   offering her perfumed hands to passers by
the boiled pineapple peel that reduces the inflammation of your ego
the guava jam   self-preserved from you

I've already been
the imprisoned servant
a teacher who mispronounces the words she attempts to teach
a mother making mistakes to avoid the mistakes her own mother made
a translator of your emotions and a clerk archiving the reports of your failures
an unseen ghost wandering the poetry venues of this city

I've already been
the hardened soil marked by all the boots going down Grand Canyon
the wind combing the bison's fur in the Plains
the tree bark in the jungle hosting orchids and bromeliads
the sunset in the Caribbean resting on your skin
the moonrise in Los Angeles without you

I've already been
a two-inch long   yellow ant
a cockatoo standing on the edge of a balcony in Caracas
a 'possum rejected for clinging too tight to the tree it climbed
a great blue heron with a broken wing after a tornado
a woman birthing herself into a trail

beautiful butterfly

by SHARNELL BLEVINS

flying, wheeling, traveling
        leaving it goes
fallen down
        trapped, captured
no pitching, no looping, not even a roll
desiring to glide above my garden
        it needs attending
trees shade the grassy dunes
sun beams engage aromatic summit blooms
        must get there, I must
reveal how to release my tethered burdens, I pray
wings coloured
        Mocha Browns,
                    Cinnamon Reigns,
                              and Coco Tans
vibrating the wind currents
shattering the frostiness
releasing the sweltering sun
while rains sweep tear stained drum
beating upon the suppressed soul
almost decimated
but
trumpets thunder, sopranos sing, basses boom
rattling the foundations
liberating hands and ankles and wings
ascending, soaring, rising
away

becoming, no, slaying,
fully who I am
always who I be
it is me recalling
it is me here
it is me flying
beautiful butterfly free

for the fir tree hanging by thin desire

written for the Misery Point Preserve, Seabeck, Washington

by CHING-IN CHEN

from Writing the Land: Windblown II Anthology

I admire your vertical ambition
you shift and settle with wind
despite falling over bluff's edge
you determined to grow up decades
straining towards cloud

I dream of you reaching in all directions
making home in this "place that is like an arm"
listening for North storms
tracking unusual impulses through crumbled dirt
watching for fallen objects making their way to shore

did you wait for your own shape to adjust
ask ocean to introduce you to cousin eelgrass
sing blessings to the forage fish

I've come to say hello today again
despite daily struggles to keep balance

I learn again from you how to re-orient back to breath, how to dream into our own roots.

A Manzanita Yad

by BONNIE S. KAPLAN

from Sinister Wisdom

I once whittled a *yad* from a fallen twig
of the manzanita bush, only I didn't
think it *yad* at the time.

As with most whittling I did not know
where I was headed. One end of the sprig
was forked, evidence of branching,

and on the other I carved a single
claw, a talon really, which tipped it
into the magical, a sorcerer's stick.

Manzanita has a natural patina
as it grows in nature and needs little
polishing, yet I sat for many

hours burnishing with a stone,
adding my own wear and shine
to an already tough and ruddy grain.

Torah and Hebrew were the farthest
thing from my mind that day in the forest,
yet something sacred was afoot.

I thought my twig a bird's perch,
a decorative fetish, not a Jewish ritual
pointer. But that is so like Judaism,

to prepare you in ways dictated
by a mystery, whispering hold on,
you will need this one day.

multiply

by ELIZABETH GALOOZIS

we have been flush
this whole time
bills folded
into one-inch squares
bound
by flaking rubber bands
buried
under a vase in pink packing peanuts

growth
has been happening
this whole time

seeds
knocked into the yard
root, bloom
pull monarchs in
on their way to Michoacán

under the hairy fig and guava branches
creepers take umbrage
wait
time in their vessels

in and under the boxes
in the closets and garage
generations of spiders
ebb and flow

there is no calm
that does not shelter
furious motion

Lizard Wish

by SUSANA GONZALES

from Gyroscope Review

I pull over safely to the side of the road
making sure to park cleanly
off the highway.
I set the parking brake,
exit after checking for oncoming traffic
and click the door lock on the key fob

and walk
and walk

into the scrub of the desert
into the wild blue sky
toward no goal
though the red rock mountain stands
before me solid and absolute

I walk until consideration falls away
I walk until propriety and dutifulness are just words
I abandon first my blouse then my binding bra
elastic and metal wire and hooks drag through the desert dirt
till it drops from the tips of my fingers

legs grow stronger browner
sinewy legs
hopscotch legs

ballerina legs
middle aged market lady legs
walk me deeper
walk me knowingly away from here

my lizard body knows what it wants
the sun on my back
the heat on my belly
a hot rock in a red desert
to lay down on
the length of my heart

Sweet Languid

By DEBORAH EDLER BROWN

She couldn't explain it, but something changed when the weather heated up. Some old part of her soul stirred, and everything slowed down. Her shadow lengthened and softened. It hid around corners. It carried gardenias. It wore a hat. It had—could it be?—a bustle. A sweet, languid shadow in those summer afternoons, lingering over lemonade and hopscotch. It didn't matter if she wore jeans or a business suit, her shadow had a hat and a bustle, carried gardenias, lingered. At first, it made her nervous, made her check for sunstroke and dehydration. But she got used to it, looked forward to its return.

The second summer she bought a hat and wore a sundress. Her shadow, sweet and languid, still had a bustle, still carried gardenias. She didn't know how she knew they were gardenias; she just knew. That June she filled a bowl with irises and experimented with perfumes from her childhood: lemon verbena, lily of the valley. The wind licked against her skin under her sundress. She bought white cotton sheets and started to sleep naked. Her shadow flirted with passing bachelors, dropped a handkerchief, a flower, let another shadow pick it up.

The men didn't notice. They were lawyers, policemen, construction workers, waiters, busy staying a step ahead of the heat, trying to stop in a breezy doorway, a bit of shade. They didn't look at what their shadows were doing. But she looked. It was better than television.

She began to take longer lunches, upped her sunscreen, broadened her hat, and watched her sweet languid shadow play coquette on the sidewalk. One day, while she read a magazine at an outside stand, her shadow had a tryst with a doctor on his lunch break and kissed a skateboarder in the park.

She was glad the summer days were long and worried about being lonely come winter. Even the nights had a touch of quiet sadness about them. But she slept early so she could get up at dawn and run, while her shadow followed on a touring bike.

She was drinking at a public fountain the day her shadow fell off its bike, and another shadow helped it up. He wore a pinstripe suit and a Panama hat and walked a dog. They talked for a long time as she stretched her calves and drank water. The man himself, a cyclist, was fixing a flat tire.

Our shadows like each other, he said, suddenly, across the grass. Would you like to have lemonade and talk about it?

She almost pulled a muscle as she whipped around to look at him. He had sweet languid eyes and, as she drew nearer, she saw the softness in his smile. She didn't know what to say, but her shadow was already in a tight embrace.

How To Fly

by TAMARA ZOOK

If you had the choice between these two superpowers, which would you choose? Being able to fly, or being invisible? Raise your internal hand.

Fly?
Invisible?

I must admit that for many years I've been very judge-y about people who chose invisible. I made up that invisible people chose invisible so they could steal things—money, ideas, people's privacy. Sorry, invisible superpower people.

I always choose flying. Wide awake or fast asleep, I've dreamed and dreamt about the ability to fly since I was little. To magically leave gravity behind, to leave the weight of my body, to travel above and beyond so quickly, so far, so effortlessly is thrilling.

I remember one of my flying dreams in grade school. I was eight or nine, flying on a very soft mattress with my head out over the edge and my arms hooked over the left and right edges of the mattress. If I wanted to go left, I dipped the left edge of the mattress, go right, dip the right edge.

When I was in college, I joined the Hang Gliding Club—in Kansas!—and we would go out to some very small, small hill, just barely a dip of a valley, and at the top of that molehill, the air would catch the wings of the hang glider. It was blissful. I was awake in this flying dream, and just like the mattress, I would dip my arm to the left and I would turn left, dip to the right and I would turn right. My feet touched the ground far too soon. In my nighttime or naptime flying dreams, I turn that molehill into a mountain and soar through the sky for seemingly ever.

I was a preacher's kid who grew up in small Kansas farm towns, and in my dreams, I went back to one town in particular: Bird City, Kansas, population 600. For 30 years after I'd left Bird City, that tiny town in an ancient buffalo wallow would pull me back, again and again. It didn't matter whether I lived in San Francisco, Philadelphia, New York City, or Los Angeles—for 30 years, my dreams took me back to Bird City. When I finally started dreaming in another location, I remember being so relieved. Surely this meant that I had grown beyond the confines of that buffalo wallow. I thought to myself. "Good job, Tamara. You're not in Bird City anymore."

There's a secret to dream flying, and I've never told anyone before. You're the first to know. There is a specific place in your brain that you have to go to in order to achieve lift off. Ready? First, you close your eyes. Now roll your eyeballs up and back into your head. Make your eyeballs feel as wide as possible while doing this. Feel that place on either side of your forehead, up into the mid-front of your brain. Can you feel the arch? It's like raising the soft palate in the back of your mouth, but this is the soft palate of your brain. Then with all your concentration, think UP! If you couldn't quite get there, try again. Close your eyes, focus your eyes wide and roll them up and into your brain. Feel the arch. Concentrate. Think UP! You are ready for lift off when your eyeballs feel like bits of a crown at the front of your head. Feel the lift?

The more you practice while you are awake, the easier it is to do in your dreams.

When you are sleeping and dreaming and happen to go to that place in your head, you will fly! You will just lift right up. Oh, wait—I forgot to tell you—when you are sleeping and dreaming and happen to go to that place in your head, you won't have to close your eyes. Eeesh, that would be really depressing if you were not able to see what you were doing—actually allowing yourself to fly! In your dreams, you can keep your eyes open and watch the ground drop away, see the tops of the trees pass in front of you and then below you, feel yourself in the blue, blue sky and have the unbelievable experience that you are indeed flying.

In a recent dream, I went back to Kansas. I was flying around the parsonage in Bird City. I'd like to be able to say I was flying around our home in Bird City, but our homes were never our own. My family never lived in a home that we thought of as ours. It was always the parsonage. It was always owned by the church, and we lived in it while my father was the minister. It was its own kind of rental agreement. In this dream, it is a warm, warm, early summer evening with a very little breeze—highly, highly unusual in windy Western Kansas. It was one of those summer evenings where the air is baby touch on your skin. My Dad and I are walking in the backyard, past the roses around to the side yard, where we have the badminton net set up so as it can't be seen much from the street so my brother and I and the rest of the neighborhood kids can play until we kill the grass and it won't matter to anyone driving by, like church parishioners who would judge my pastor father about how he was taking care of the lawn. My father was nothing if not meticulous about the parsonage lawn. At least the part that could be seen from the street. Appearances count.

Dad and I are walking around to this side yard, and in an unusual act of confidence and desire to connect with my normally disinterested father, I say, "Look, Dad, I can fly." I proceed to fly up to the roof of the parsonage, and as I stand there on the parsonage roof looking down on my father, he says matter-of-factly "Well, I guess you can." I see my father seeing me, as if for the first time, and for the first time, I understand why being invisible doesn't feel like a superpower to me, and from my perch on the parsonage roof, I again find that place in my brain, feel the arch and think UP!

Overmade

by ANDREA AUTEN

Two older women sat under Francine's driers, their hair in rollers, sour looks thrown my way. *Keep walking, face front, eyes over their heads.* Magazines fanned out across the front counter gleamed in the morning sun. I welcomed the shiny covers. Lady Di hairstyles, Lady Di fashions. Whose wedding dress design would she wear, how many pounds would her wedding crown weigh. She'd be Princess Diana seven days from today. But the hairstyle and fashion magazines were meant for paying customers only. I shifted from the glaring women and picked out a package of pink curlers.

Two miles walking in old leather flats had landed me in our one-stop-sign downtown. I had a list burning in my skirt pocket. Small items for a new life: lip gloss, tampons, tissues, and questions. Empty shops relieved me. Not much to see around here, anyway. No always-there folks, no laughter behind me, no hearing, "There's that ate-up and spit-out Lizbeth." Tired of this town that never gave to me, tired from the long walk, just tired. Nineteen years old and still this. I stopped at a manhole cover and imagined myself being pulled down under. Big-storm water still rushed under the streets, making the pipes sound more like a river. Water taking the long way to The Great Mississippi.

I had headed over to McKinley Drug fixed on my getaway plan when the smell of hairspray stopped me in front of Francine's. I'd avoided styling shops. All those women. Couldn't imagine giving my hair over to anyone other than my mama, Gin. Her blunt chops on the porch steps held me over until I took to cutting my own ends.

But as I stood there, the entrance seemed to call to me. A way to break the sameness of my life. Women did it every day. Came in and walked out new. What could it be, having people do for me as I did for everybody else? Down to changing baby diapers at work, I was a hands-on do-for-others woman. Someone else combing through my hair, buffing my nails, pressing down my tight shoulders until the chest breathed deep. I could enter this place quick and see what went on inside. Nerves flickered in my belly, I'd made myself walk forward.

"Be right there, love," Francine called now. A woman I'd known and never talked to, Francine seemed to be easy company. A bubbling babbler, hair dyed like Sunday black shoes, wide belt cinched around a smock, holding in her big middle. Able to balance on heels, standing all day, popping her gum, and patting clients on their shoulders. She picked out a client's last few white curls and clouded the head in hairspray. When the old lady rose from the chair, no small feat getting those brittle bones to a stand, they hugged and said goodbye. Francine pocketed a fold of cash.

I stood straighter and made room for the old maid leaving the shop. This woman I knew but didn't want to; my fourth-grade teacher who'd dogged me for one-hundred-eighty miserable days. Memories still burned. "Goodbye, Miss Tunney," I said. Her face twitched out a smirk.

I paged through more beauty magazines. Deeper in the stack, I saw Lady Di in June's edition of *People*, her hair catching the light in chunks of butter yellow. Bangs bent across her forehead. The future princess shimmered, pink-cheeked in a red polka dot jacket and a high neck white blouse. I set the curlers down and pulled the magazine close. The pages inside revealed how Lady Diana had six wedding gowns made special.

Plastic fingernails clicked near my head. "Sunshine, what can I do you for today?"

"I, uh…what are, what is the price?" I held up sponge rollers.

"Depends," Francine said. "$40 for a cut and color, $20 for a cut only and either choice will get you the curlers for free or you can just take those curlers for $2.50."

The curlers had pink specks glittering the sponges. Candy to my eyes.

"Them curlers wouldn't put a dent in your hair though." Francine reached up high and lifted my ponytail. "Tangled holly bush you got in there."

A laugh chopped out of me, loud as a gun. "I'm sorry," I whispered. "Never had my hair done formal before and don't suppose I'll do it now."

Francine cooed, "Well, let's suppose you do. Can't hurt none. Why don't you set up at my station over there? Read that magazine and let me cut and color you for the price of what you can spare. You got time? It'll be about 3 hours. Maybe a tad more."

I had fifteen dollars. At least ten dollars was needed for getaway items. A cut like Lady Di and blonde color. Doable, if I worked another shift at the St. George's infant room and brought back what I owed. I took to reasoning, making a case to the jury in my head: Had meat in the oven slow-cooking back home. Gin was off with that New Man. My stomach flipped over. A hairdo taken right from the cover of a magazine. I could be ready for the big city. The need grabbed tight. I rotated the cover until it faced Francine and pointed.

I feared she'd laugh, but this was Francine. Always more than kind. My feet tingled, ready to sprint. Lady Di stared up at me, telling me, *yes*.

"$40 is more than I got."

Francine laced her candy red nails through cutting sheers. "Couldn't hurt to give you some layering. A little style. March right over here." We stopped at a chair that looked too small to hold me.

"Plop on down and I'll lower you with my foot pump."

Francine got me wrapped, caped, and snapped. She misted my hair while talking to the lady one chair over. My hair frothed into silver beads after rain. Francine lowered a hood over my head and tied it under my chin. Fear stared me back in the mirror, or maybe hope. Stupid girl sitting here spending money I didn't have to become a Lady Di knock-off.

A crochet hook dove into the hood and plucked. Francine pulled strands through a tiny hole. She repeated the act, quickly, expertly. I winced with every pull of that awful hook speeding across my scalp. Hair sprouted out from the cap, looking electrified.

Was the smell skunk? I couldn't look up once that cap took over. But Lady Di stared up from my lap as if to tell me I could achieve beauty. Her blue-lined eyes almost winked. Francine slopped cold goop onto the cap. Seems she helped it along by brushing stiff hits into the cap. I followed her to a drier. Each step itching under the cap. Every move embarrassing.

"Here's the magazine stack you were thumbing through. Want some Russian Tea? I have a fresh jar. Wyler's Lemonade, Tang, sugar, and Nestea. You'll love it." I barely nodded before she trawled off.

What secrets did Francine keep about every woman in this town? What did she hear about mine? Francine would know Gin's constant parade of men and the seesaw love she rode with them.

I paged through each magazine as my hair crisped under the drier. A terrible hot singed my ears. I pressed back into the seat. Hair driers must be made for smaller women. I sank low as I could, shrank away from the dome. One hand holding down magazines, the other clamping the mug handle, I sipped hot liquid. Orange bitter mixed with sweet-sour. The high life sitting right here. Not a care.

"Let's wash you out." Jolted by her voice, I let every magazine slide to the floor. "Leave those. We'll get them. Follow me to the sinks and set yourself at my station."

Too much mirror to face. I stared at my knees. "You need thinned out," Francine said. "Never had it before, I can tell, but you trust me now." Seemed Francine caught my worries. But a hairdo had me less nervous than explaining how I only had half the price of her charge in my pocket. Money already spoken for. Combing and snipping, talking, laughing, now and then Francine pushed on my shoulder when she said a piece of something juicy. I slipped my hands under my thighs and kept a grin pasted on. "How much longer you think?"

"Oh, not long. You got a date?"

The air thickened around me. Hairspray, humming women, heat rising. This is the time women talk to each other. Back and forth, comfortable chatter about kids and dogs, gardens, and parties. Easy peasy talk about nothing. I'd been kept young, careful, and quiet for nineteen years, but I had an untold plan and learning all I could fast took hold. "Francine, can you answer me something?" My voice sounded small, unsure.

"Well, I'll certainly try. What you want to know?"

"You own this business, right?"

Her face beamed. "I do. Twenty-five years next month. Wanna buy it?"

Couldn't even buy this cut and color. I cowered under her comb tearing through my hair. "What's a W-2?" I let go of the breath I didn't know I was holding.

"That's just a form your boss gives you for taxes. You need a job first. You looking for one?" Scissored bits of bang sprinkled my cheeks. "I know everybody. What kinda work you like?" Up close, I could see the face powder settling in the creases of her doll face.

"No ... thank you ... no, I have a job. I tend babies and toddlers at St. George's up the highway. I don't get those W-2s though. I'm paid in cash."

Francine's face twitched. Just the slightest frown between her eyebrows. "I know the place," she said. Not too kindly either. But just as quick, she smiled again and brushed her fingers across my forehead. "They're required to give you a W-2 once a year come January. It's a record; the hours you worked. You might get a check back from the government, you might have to pay them. Should tell you all this when you was hired."

I nodded. My muscles ached for sitting this long. Regret creeping in. My family needed me home. Francine curled and sprayed, combed and fussed over me. I prepared myself. Hope can be a driver of the dumbest choices. Deep breaths, time to face the mirror. Eyes up.

I gasped at the strange me looking back.

"Didn't I say you could trust me?"

Light yellow, every curl in order, closer to my head, the wires all tamed. "I love it. Francine, I really love it." I fumbled from under the cape to produce my purse. When I turned money out of it, $15 spread in my lap. I couldn't look up from the crumpled bills, couldn't think of what to say, or how to fix the fact that I needed much of what I had. "I'm short," I whispered.

"Next time, honey. You run on now." She took the $5 only.

The V.F.W. hall clock said the afternoon had stolen away. I stopped to take in my disbelief. Four hours gone as if they were minutes. Hours answering to nobody. Stiff back, hungry, I walked with a bounce. Caught my hairdo in the drugstore window. "I can't believe it's me," I said to the image smiling back and circled to face the shops across the street.

A lady floated out of Preston's Hardware. She stopped, but three feet from me, and surveyed the sky. After turning her perfect hair into the breeze, she sifted through her purse, pulled out a bonnet and tied it to her chin. I tried not to stare.

Handbag open, white gloves pulled out, I studied how the woman slipped them onto perfect hands. Perfume sweetened the air between us.

One step into the street, she stopped again and looked. Satisfied the road was empty, the walk began. A model walk, one ankle notched in front of the other, unmarked white heels pride-stepping on our dirty street. She avoided puddles without even looking. When she reached the other side, she lifted up onto the sidewalk and posed just outside Ida's Diner. I was beauty-struck, left frozen and watching. She fished out sunglasses and placed them on her face. This rare and perfect woman didn't fit in my faded town.

Who did she belong to in this one-stoplight-end-of-the-line? She smoothed her gloves over slim hips and ran them the length of her narrow skirt. Breath warmed my lower lip until I tamped my mouth shut.

The woman opened a small mirror and checked the angle of her bangs. Every move was practiced, cotillion queen, taught by mothers, aunts, and wealthy widows. Southern royalty, a Lady Di in West Tennessee.

Two girls slipped out front, waving back at the baker. I stood still only long enough to watch the jean-skirts-with-matching-jean-jacket sisters greet the mystery lady. The woman knelt, full of sugary kindness, and snuggled littler sister, then stood up and straightened big sister's collar. Their mother, a beauty queen. She took each daughter's hand in hers and walked to the corner.

Before they could cross back my way, I turned and rushed for the alley behind McKinley Drug. Each quick step jarred my back. I hid at the dumpsters, then forced myself out through the metal odor of dead meat mixed with beer bottle sick sweet, wet cardboard stacks rain-pounded to sour mush. I cleared the backs of the main street businesses and ran without turning back.

A breeze stirred our porch swing. I took in one more breath and readied for whatever came. Peeled off my muddy shoes, set them on the top stair, and waited on the porch. Not wanting to shock my great-granny, I patted my hair and pushed bangs from my eyes. *Put hairspray on the list.* Best choice was to walk in the front room and march to the pot on the stove, all business. I accepted this, pulled back the screen and walked inside.

The smell of good meat filled each corner, dampening the air that left a misty film on every surface. Barefoot, I slipped into the kitchen and busied with the meal. Serving dishes set on old potholders, steam curling, I rummaged for water glasses. The best three of the cruddy lot. Extended, reaching through shelves, my hands were long, pretty things. I marveled at them, moving through the air, grasping a serving spoon. Lovely finger lines not of me, but beyond me. Hands carved at the start of what God intended and got lost. I twirled the spoon. *Look at me.* Suddenly royal, I turned and pointed the scepter while lowering at the knee to an invisible presence, tucked my chin and slowly rose. Proud, I bounced the stiff curls in my left palm. Lady Lizbeth, reigning head of the crooked cabin.

"What on earth?" Great Granny interrupted.

I snapped the wave back.

"What have you done to yourself? Spent money to join the circus? Trying to be Marilyn Monroe. Who for?"

I gripped the serving spoon harder. My face bulged in the metal. Bright lemon curls frizzing over my ear. I jammed my eyes closed to bring back Lady Di. She helped straighten my back to a royal position. My neck became long and thin and my legs were slender and perfectly shaped. My body turned into the pretty mother who cupped her arms around Big sister and Little Sister. The girls smiled at me with bridal white teeth, flashing in the sunlight.

"You listening to me? Don't take your mother's path."

I kept my eyes closed tight, tried to stay with Lady Di, but her image crumbled. I returned to robot. Plate, fork, knife, and spoon times three, set the table.

Startled by a sudden clang, I shot my chin toward the door. Gin swung open the screen and danced circles into the room. She teetered over her knees, dipped a low curtsy, and spun back to that New Man holding open the screen door. She turned to wink my way then froze.

"What in the Sam Hell—"

New Man who never said much spoke so deep the windows liked to rumble. "You've changed your hair. It's lovely," he boomed. "What's the name of the color?"

"Fool's gold," Great-Granny Bee called out.

"Wait. What is this?" Gin said. Her voice locked into high gear. "What fool's gold decision did you make?" All sirens now. "You're embarrassing me—how did you pay for it?"

New Man counted his fingers.

"Answer me. How did you pay for this stupid choice? You look cheap."

Face flaring red, New Man grasped the screen door handle.

Gin moved in, examined me close, and sniffed. "Don't wait up." Then I heard it, small and mean. A laugh under Gin's breath. She patted my hairdo, whipped her heels across the linoleum, grabbed her pocketbook from the side table, and walked to the held door.

New Man said, "Good night, ladies."

Out into the fading light the two of them walked, arms linked at the elbows. The screen slammed behind them and just as that metal clanked shut, a word clicked in my brain. *Now.* I sailed to the bedroom, knelt hard-knee on the floor, ignoring Great Granny Bee's protests. Reached harder and pulled out my getaway bag. *Run where nobody knows you.* I hoisted up onto the bed, *run past the river,* and jammed my hand down into the dusty mouth. *Run to the bus line,* fished, and fumbled, tore away the carefully placed clothes, and when I located the thin cash roll, I squeezed it tight. *Go.*

Great Granny Bee leaned into the recliner, her chest heaving. Determined Irish, withered face, her fountain of unending love. We breathed goodbye.

Back out in the hot night, itching yellow prickling hair, I stepped lighter, shoes in hand, bag swinging with each foot forward. Out, beyond, into the never-here-again.

Stay in My Corner

BY ANGELA FRANKLIN

My religious dad had me tethered
tight to his Southern roots and ribs
with biblical restrictions.

Still, I gathered guts to ask,
Daddy, can I go to the party down the block?
We'll see, he said, not looking
up from the newspaper.

My teenage will heard *Yes.*
All week I practiced smooth dance moves,
chose clothes to wear, did my hair,
laundry, dusting and dishes.

Daddy, the party is tonight. Can I still go?

He put down LA Times, looked
into my eyes and said *Nope.*

But Daddy, it's only three doors down.
You said I could go.

When did I say you could go? I said
We'll see. But I didn't promise.

Daddy, I never get to do nothing!
Everybody else is going. Why can't I?

I then hatched plans to defy my dad,
placed a dummy in the bed,
perched a wig on its head,
escaped restrictions through bedroom window.

Disobedience waxed electric dressed
in bellbottom slacks, Nehru jacket,
chains gold medallion dangling,
I flipped a quarter at the door,

Floated into dusty garage scented
with mean mixes of motor oil and cheap cologne.
Tyrone and Jerome had morphed a shack
into a funky Black American Bandstand.

Dashikis shimmied, mile high afros
bobbed and weaved to slick guitar licks.
We camel-walked and did the splits
to *Say it Loud, I'm Black and I'm Proud.*

Clever DJ slowed the pace
placed *Stay in My Corner* on turntable,
that 1968 slow drag doo-wop harmony hit.

I was feeling way past 15 clutched
in arms of a cute boy
as falsetto soloist crooned

Stay .... staaaaay... wooo hoo wa haa.

I swooned until a chorus said
Hey, Angie, yo daddy want you.

Cloaked in cobalt light, I ignored warnings, dizzy
from Hai Karate aftershave, thought they were lying.

Suddenly, someone was trying to cut in.
Dry calloused fingertips tapped my neck.
I spun around and looked
up at my big tall dad. Bug-eyed

visions of leather and switches on legs and backside
sucked residue of freedom from feet now wobbly with fear.

On the way home
I gathered guts again
and said to him,
Daddy, I know you're going
to whop me, but I just want
you to know I had a very good time.

He never beat me again.

i wish church felt like *this*

by CARLY MARIE DEMENTO

i would enter you.
consensually, of course.
not your physical border
but the tide line.
i would like to meet you there
as if we were dying, our distillate
a tumble of images and thank yous.
i would like to meet you as water, inchoate dream.
no, i don't mean the twinkle in your mother's eye.
i mean, when the universe first dreamed
you. i would like to meet you
at the tip of your tongue
the edge of blossom. before
what you say becomes
the small artifact
of who you are.
i would like to name you
            huge
and sit with that one.
right here.
yes, right here.
i speak to a roaring ocean.

The Urge

By TIMEA SIPOS

It's been about two days since I crawled inside Pete's chest. That's what I figure, since there were several hours where his heartbeat slowed to a dull, even thumping at the back of my head. His veins wrap around me like a loosely knit cardigan, and during that time the blood in them changed from a heavy rush to an easy flow. At first, I thought he'd laid down again because he was exhausted from lugging me around. Then his breathing steadied. Up to then his lungs were like life jackets muffling my ears. They deflated to small pillows. I was suddenly afraid he was dying. Then, when his breaths didn't get any shallower and his heartbeat didn't get any softer, I realized he must be asleep.

This and the number of his bowel movements are the only ways I have to tell time in here. So far, I've felt the food he's eaten work its way through his intestines, compact itself, and exit his colon twice. It's such an intimate feeling every time that I almost forget to be disgusted.

I didn't exactly plan to crawl inside Pete's chest. I just get this urge sometimes when we're holding each other in bed or when I'm kissing him to get as much of me inside of him as possible. Like I could suffocate him and it still wouldn't be enough.

I've always been this way. During the first weekend we ever spent together I remember I straddled his chest, folded my head into his neck and just cried. I knew I'd never have to feel lonely ever again. He asked what was wrong, but it was too soon for me to say it, so I just said, It's been a long time since I felt this way. He stroked my hair and laid kisses on my temple.

The only time I ever feel truly and completely whole is when he's inside me, and I only remember that once he pulls out and I'm left empty again, painfully aware of where he ends and I begin, and the space between the two. I was so sick of that feeling. The last time he was inside me, I was determined to do everything possible to avoid the pain of him leaving me. Which is how I ended up here. Inside of him.

He was on top of me, moving with long, slow strokes when I felt the urge building, mistaking it at first for an orgasm, and I could sense where this would go if I gave in. His hair cast a shadow across his face as it fell over his eyes, so that I couldn't see any worry in it, only the satisfaction in his trembling lip. I pressed myself into him harder, coating his skin with my skin, the oil of me waxing the marble floor of him, careful to breathe in only when he breathed out. We rolled over so that he was on his back, and as I adjusted, he pressed my head into his chest, a maternal but rough movement, the way an ape presses her young to her breast. I cracked his chest open. He let out a sharp cry, but it could have been just as much from pleasure as from pain. I could feel his dick grow harder inside me. That was all the reassurance I needed. I parted his ribs with my hands, like opening a theater curtain, and crawled inside him.

I guess you could say I love hard. Pete calls it destructive. He begs me to be softer. Like when I give him a bear hug after he gets home from work, and he says he almost swallowed his tongue. Or when I kiss him so hard he says I almost knock his teeth out. It's not intentional. I just can't help it. I imagine he's afraid of the damage my love could do to him in here. Like I could grab his heart and clutch it until my fingernails puncture the chambers. He'd bleed out and I'd drown in his blood. Unless I choked on it first.

Actually, I think he's often being dramatic. I think he secretly treasures the intensity of my love. I think he pretends it's too much because it's embarrassing for him when I lose control. I mean, it has to make him feel good to know I'm willing to give up my friends, my job—which I can't stand but helps pass the time until

Pete comes home—the dandelions outside my office window, the taste of coffee in the mornings, everything, just to be inside him. But still, he keeps up this act, because after all these years he still doesn't feel like he deserves me.

That's why I can be too much for him sometimes, I know that. Like when he's getting ready for work and I hide his keys so he can stay with me and he gets annoyed and wants to spank me for it and I take the red marks on my behind because it means I can have ten more minutes with him. Or when I shut off the breaker on game night and fake a power outage so we can spend time together by candlelight. But when it's playoff season and he doesn't want to miss the game so he decides to watch it at the bar and is searching for his keys in the dark, I often think that if I were inside him, like I most want to be when I'm holding him tight, we'd never have to be apart.

That's why I was so thrilled to finally crawl inside him. Once I settled in, I let out a long, warm sigh, and he said, Don't you get comfortable in there now, and I said, But it's just so soft and mushy, I could stay in here forever, oh yes I could!

Ha-ha, very funny, he said in that scolding tone of his that makes me feel like a child, but one who's cared for.

C'mon, I said, *this* is intimacy. Don't you want to be intimate with me?

And it turned out he did want to be intimate, because he left me alone for a while, went about his day, even took me down to the bodega for snacks. I could feel his abdominals contracting as he climbed back up the stairs. Afterwards, he made sure I was okay by stroking his belly. I pressed my palms against his so I could feel them more, and I wondered if he could see the outline of my fingers under his skin. In this way, we've evolved beyond words.

I feel his lungs rise and fall beside my ears, the contractions of his intestines below me as they push the bodega chips through in waves, and the tightening of his muscles all around me with each movement he makes. I listen to the whirr of his blood as it carries oxygen through his veins, throughout his whole body, working overtime to expel the carbon dioxide I breathe into him. It's nice to feel that his body is willing to do extra work to keep me comfortable in here.

That is, until I feel a sharp stab in my uterus. My period. Two days early. As I shed my blood inside him, I'm overwhelmed by the idea that I'm actively changing his bio-chemistry to better reflect mine. Like I'm stamping him with my blood. I've always wanted kids with Pete, but this is so much better! I want to tell him that his body is changing, that it's fusing with mine, but I decide to keep it to myself. At least for a time. Like how a woman guards the early news of her pregnancy. I sit with the secret. I even think about what it would be like if I were pregnant. How his stomach would expand along with mine. We'd look like one of those Russian dolls. The fantasies lead me into a warm and cocooned sleep.

Later, I wake to the walls of Pete's abdominals closing in on me. Below me are several hard objects, jabbing my back, ass, and thighs. For an instant, I think my womb is falling out of me. Pete lets out a guttural noise I mistake at first to be my own. Then, when I feel the first hard clump exit his body the way a boulder might roll down a flight of stairs, I recognize that it's the chips giving him grief on their way out. Pete's always had trouble digesting processed foods.

The last series of contractions around me are violent enough to make my cramps pick up again. I hear the hushed scream of the toilet and feel Pete's lungs inflate-deflate-inflate as he pants, but my own contractions are just beginning. They're intense enough that I can't help but let out a groan. Had enough? Pete asks, the first he's spoken to me today. His voice sounds so muffled to me in here that initially I think he says, Alright, muffin? I pull my knees closer to my chest, and as I do, I can hear sucking sounds near my elbow as the skin of my arm stretches and pulls. Trying to peel my arm away from Pete's liver is like trying to remove a swarm of leeches from my body. I'm happy to know his body is accepting me like a successfully transplanted organ. With time, he will need me to function just like I've always needed him.

The cramps get so bad I think about asking him to take an ibuprofen so I can suck it out of his stomach. As I shift to move, riding out another wave, my foot slips down into his large intestine. Pete lets out a groan, and we tip forward. Blood rushes to my head—the blood in his body, the blood in my brain, all of it.

What the hell? he says, equal parts anger and fear.

Shit. I'm so sorry, baby.

I don't know which part of him to caress. I push my cheek against his stomach, and the metallic taste of blood quickly fills my mouth. Our blood now, I smile to myself. I wiggle my toes to pet whatever I kicked, and when I do, the head of my foot slips inside a small cavity at the end of which I can unmistakably feel his prostate with my big toe.

Not now, he says, That really hurt. I pretend not to hear him, making concentric circles with my left toe and kneading periodically. Things swell down there. My foot is wedged securely, so the swelling compresses it enough to keep it warm but not so much that I don't have room to continue. The motion is a good distraction from my pain. Pete's heart rate climbs up and up. I tilt my head to the right, so that his heart quits tapping the back of my skull. His abdominals contract in off-rhythm beats now, so I know he's close.

All in all, it doesn't take long for Pete to come. When he does, he lets out a moan unlike any I've heard from him before. His groin pumps so hard it lifts my foot several inches up, then back down. Meanwhile, something like a jolt of electricity runs up his spine. It's powerful enough to numb my cramps.

Damn, he breathes. We both pant, a big breath inside an even bigger breath. I can picture beads of sweat decorating his forehead and chest. No matter how warm and safe I feel in here, I have to admit I'm starting to miss seeing Pete from the outside, feeling his hands on my skin.

And just as I'm thinking about his fingers gliding between my legs, I sense the unmistakable smell of smoke. No, he wouldn't, I think. Not with me in here.

I'd suspected Pete had picked up smoking again. I've smelled it on him some nights after he's come home from the bar with his friends, but I didn't think his addiction had gotten so serious again.

My eyes sting until they water, like I just swam for hours in a chlorinated pool. Pete! Seriously?! As I open my mouth to speak, I suck in what seeps out of his lungs. I hack and cough, my body shaking his organs like sticky alarm bells until I'm dizzy.

C'mon, babe, live a little, he says. I can hear the smirk in his voice. *This* is intimacy. Be intimate with me.

Don't make me crawl out of here and smack that smile off your face!

Oh, I wish you would.

I fold my arms across my chest, jabbing my elbow into his diaphragm.

He grunts, smoke catching in his trachea. He coughs until both our lungs are hot.

Had enough? I ask. And he must've, because the smoke stops seeping into his chest cavity. My eyes keep watering though. They spill over the rim of my lids and now I'm sobbing, my shoulders shaking and everything. I've never felt so far away from Pete.

It seems like he wants me out at all costs. No matter what new heights of pleasure I can bring him to from in here.

I'm thinking about what it might mean for me to climb out when another stream of smoke enters Pete's trachea. What spills out of his lungs this time is not the dry smell of burning tobacco but the sweet, almost sour stench of marijuana. Pete knows that of the two times I've tried weed, I threw up once and another time fell into a paralyzing sleep.

I can't believe how irresponsible you're being, I say.

He leans back on the couch. Everything shifts and contorts inside him so that I lean back with him. Carrying you around is exhausting, he says. I deserve to unwind a little.

I don't buy it. I think he feels exposed. I can see too much of him from in here. What he does when I'm normally not around. I think he wants to subdue me so he can remove me.

You know, you don't have to smoke me out, I say. I can come out without you drugging me. Less a plea and more an announcement.

Are you saying you'll come out now if I put out this joint? He sounds more forgiving than I expected.

I close my eyes and focus on how his chest cavity envelops me, how his organs hold me tighter than he ever did. Almost with the same intensity I hold him when I'm outside him. I think about how the blood that runs here is half mine now, the DNA just as much a reflection of him as me, the organs dependent on my presence to hold them in place, so what right does he have to kick me out, really?

So? He asks.

I hold my breath and plug my nostrils with my thumb and forefinger, jamming my elbows into his ribs, preparing for what's to come. A long pillar of smoke filters down Pete's trachea, less like the hit of a joint and more like a bong rip. If he can handle it, so can I.

Let's live a little.

Stunning Vistas

by RAMONA REEVES

from Barely South Review

The law says you can marry another woman.

The woman you marry will not be the retired math teacher you met for coffee. She dropped a scourge of keys and a folding wallet onto the glass table at the coffee shop and stared at your brown leather purse as though it might implode. "I like costumes," she said. "I make pink tutus for a festival in the spring." You soon learned tutus would be attendees' sole festival apparel.

The woman you marry could not be the one espousing membership in that other political party, the one that would never allow you to marry in the first place. "On social issues I'm with you," she said, "but fiscally I must vote the other way." She droned on about Abe Lincoln for what felt like fourscore and seven years and cringed at the word lesbian.

The woman you marry will not be the insurance attorney so deep in the closet you needed a detective to find her, especially when she quite literally took the fifth the day after tonguing you so hard you pondered ethics and the law as it applies to making out.

Nor will the woman you marry be the athlete who coached you about muscle groups and food. She cardio-walked and carbed-up, ran marathons, triathlons and lifted weights; her t-bands were often out of whack. You imagined couching-to-5K for the rest of your life.

Neither is the woman you'll marry the gluten-free librarian with OCD and a fear of loud noises. "Ligyrophobia is a big problem," she said. "Motorcycles terrorize me." You consider the Honda Rebel 450 and Slingerland drums you once owned, your barking dog and the enthusiasm you exhibit for your favorite sports team in the fall.

The woman you marry will not be the one who swore she looked like Linda Ronstadt, but when you met, more resembled Gene Simmons. You wouldn't have minded the female version of Simmons. It's just that delusion is not a quality you value in a partner.

The woman you marry will not be the one who messaged for months in that dating app and canceled every face-to-face. She was interesting and knew how to spell, but it's difficult to imagine a future with someone you never see.

And the woman you marry is not the one you loved, the one who taught you friendship is sometimes the better of two lakes: one prone to drop-offs and no-swimming signs, the other a place you float free. The woman you marry won't be her, although she taught you about the woman you will marry, the one beyond your original and small concept of love, beyond the fears that once built squalls of fire around your heart. The one you will marry packages and presents your beauty with your faults. "For you, my love," she says.

Together you will climb to an enchanted place, and nearly breathless, you'll reach the bald summit and marvel at ravines and stunning vistas below. Somewhere in the distance are families who approve, churches that don't judge and a country open to all.

"Selfie?" you'll ask, and the two of you will stand with your backs to the vastness of what is, your faces cheek to cheek as you store this moment with the tap of one finger, to prove it was worth the climb, to prove she was worth the wait, to prove you were here.

Enrollment Form in Gujarati

by SAHARE WAZIRALI

I am responsible if my baby nephew cannot read or—sure, I'll turn it into a poem.

> Critical period. Bells ringing.
> Bills pile on roach filled tops.
> AI can guess which shoes she wants but for classes cannot
>   sign her up.
> An immigrant, her child, has
> has more to worry about than just
> green cards.

Frozen Yogurt After School and his Green Goblin costume, for example.

> To start a life over
> within a life

The shame we hide within our rhymes
of mangoes and curry
of partition and the like.

I reflect the truth into a stanza or just let it be. Either way my nephew will know the master when he peers into the mirror, shining bright and yellow teeth.

august 14

by SAHARE WAZIRALI

Vande Mataram the ball in the sky
lights orange and green
white stamp at the center.

Hindi speaks over
Malayalam and Telugu.
A mustache waves a flag
the country that gave his family life
liberty
loss and being found again,
only three generations later.

Only three generations ago
our mothers lost their sons.
Then they lost their sons
unclean water
unvaccinated maggots.
Stop procreating, globe on fire,
they tell us.

The Tejano band restarts.
Aquí estamos.
Since God knows when.

Chicana, Zapoteca, Gujarati, Punjabi
Land we litter with labels we need cause
We won't be forgotten.

Resilience, Resistance, Community, Expression, Healing

By MARIE CARTIER

CHARACTERS

PROTAGONIST (NARRATOR)

SETTING

The stage is empty, with a single spotlight illuminating the protagonist as they deliver their monologue.

PROTAGONIST

(Recalling a time when their resilience surprised them.)

Can I recall a time when my resilience surprised me? My mother always said, "If you feel bad, go out into the garden and eat worms." Sigh. We didn't have a garden. My resilience. *(Pauses)* My head hits the counter, as my father's hand slams into the back of my head. I am locked in a closet. I am. That would be my mother as I grew up. Kicked up. Weeds grow. They do. What is surprising to me at sixty is not my resilience, but the fact that I never leaned back. Stopped. Being resilient is the inside and out of my blood type—moving through all of my veins. I am surprised if I cut myself there is blood left. But there is. I still bleed.

(Pauses, reflecting)

(Recalling a time when resistance was the only option)

Can I recall a time when resistance was the only option? My father. I am twelve. My best friend is over. I go in the other room with him. I have to. She hears this, my best friend. I resist shame like a knife blade I hold. I leave the room with the blade held out. Shame then holds out a cloak promising me something. A space to hide maybe. I resist. I am in a cold fever. My best friend and I sit; we are watching a documentary on TV. My mother sits behind us. She says to no one, "Things happen at everyone's house. I bet things happen at your house, too." My best friend and I say nothing. I resist feeling. On the TV are flamingos, and I will hate flamingos for the rest of my life.

(Pauses, deep in thought)

(Recalling a time when community saved them.)

Recall a time when community saved you. I re-attach myself to that room, thirty years ago ... five hundred or more strong. We are gathered to hear new authors talk about a new book, Courage to Heal. The authors, Ellen and Laura, come to the edge of the stage, so close they almost step out of the light. Ellen says, "You do not have to forgive your perpetrator in order to heal." A roar inside of me echoes and bursts and stands up in the room with the roar bursting from everyone in the room. Incest survivors. We all are standing up and we are all roaring. We are. We are seen. We see each other. We are—enough. I am held and I am there. We are together in that healing. That spell. I was there and I was healed.

(Pauses, recalling the moment)

(Reflecting on how their expression shifted)

How has your expression shifted? I read poetry in bars before people read poetry, before slams, before it was called spoken word. I yelled from the stage to two guys talking in front of me, "Hey! I'm reading poetry up here!" I yelled until all conversation stopped, and I was reading into a silence that held me. I said I was raped. I was hit. But I was here now. I was speaking. I said I was told not to tell, but I was talking. I was telling—it all. I spoke and moved and was. And I saw the people in the bar raise their glasses; the two guys were back in the room toasting me. And I bowed. I was and I am. I do poetry. I do it in the fire of my belly. My truth. It's not right or wrong how one learns to speak. But ... I did learn. I opened my mouth and yelled, and I was heard. And I healed.

(Pauses, remembering the power of expression)

(Recalling what helped through periods of suffering)

What helped through periods of suffering? As a young girl, I would go outside, and I would find a garter snake, a green snake, and I would wind it around my ankle, and I would go into the woods with the snake around my ankle. I would lie under blueberry bushes and strip the berries into my mouth. I would build a tree fort four stories high and climb to where no one could go. I would swing so high on the backyard swing I was level with the ground. I would tie on skates and skate for miles on the river. I would go, climb, ride as fast as I could. And then I would go further. As far as I could go. And then further. And as I moved, I found people. My friends, my tribe, my pod. They were not garter snakes, but they were good. They were there.

(Pauses, reminiscing)

(Softly)

I have a deep love and respect for snakes. I will always love snakes, and I hold out hope for that snake I found so many days when I was a young girl running for my life.

(Pauses, reflective)

(With conviction)

I make it so. And, to every person who pulled me up, rather than slapped me down, I still see you. I still feel you, and I still hear you.

(Pauses, gratitude)

(Softly, with a touch of wonder.)

If you've never felt the body of a snake, you probably don't know that it is cool and dry. It is soft and silky. A snake in the grass saved me.

(Pauses, letting the words sink in)

(With strength)

Lilith in the Tree of Wisdom whispered to me, "Tell your truth and you will find your way out. Find your story, and you can get the hell out of here."

(Looking directly at the audience.)

And she was right.

PROTAGONIST takes a deep breath, holding a moment of silence. Lights fade gradually, leaving the PROTAGONIST in darkness.

CURTAIN falls slowly.

CONTRIBUTORS

Erika Ayón emigrated from Mexico when she was five years old and grew up in South Central Los Angeles. She graduated from UCLA with a B.A. in English. She is a former PEN Emerging Voices Fellow. She has taught poetry to middle and high school students across Los Angeles. Her work has appeared in *The Acentos Review, Chiricú Journal, Wide Awake Anthology, Coiled Serpent Anthology*, and elsewhere. Her debut poetry collection *Orange Lady* received Honorable Mention for Poetry at the 2019 International Latino Book Awards.

Li Yun Alvarado is the author of *Words or Water*. Her work has appeared in *The Acentos Review*; *VIDA Review*; *Raising Mothers*; *Coiled Serpent: Poets Arising from the Cultural Quakes & Shifts of Los Angeles*; *Aster(ix)*; and *Wise Latinas: Writers on Higher Education*; among others. She has served as the Senior Poetry Editor for *Kweli Journal* and is an alumna of VONA/Voices Writing Workshop and AROHO. Li Yun is a native New Yorker living with her husband and kids in California who misses regular trips back to Salinas, Puerto Rico to visit the rest of la familia. www.liyunalvarado.com.

Andrea Auten is a cross-genres writer based in Los Angeles. She holds two master's degrees in creative writing, one from Antioch University Los Angeles where she teaches creative writing and works as a writing specialist. Her work has been featured in *Emerge Literary Journal, Lady/Liberty Lit, Lunch Ticket, The Antioch Voice*, and in *Made in L.A.'s* third anthology, and she is a dual host of *The Scapegoat Guild* podcast. She lives with her husband and their two cats. Andrea can be found at: andreaauten.com.

Xochitl-Julisa Bermejo is the author of *Posada: Offerings of Witness and Refuge* (Sundress Publications) and *Incantation: Love Poems for Battle Sites* (Mouthfeel Press). A former Steinbeck Fellow and Poets

& Writers California Writers Exchange winner, she's received residencies from Hedgebrook, Ragdale, Yefe Nof, and National Parks Arts Foundation in partnership with Gettysburg National Military Park and Poetry Foundation. Her poem "Battlegrounds" was featured at Academy of American Poets' Poem-a-Day, On Being's *Poetry Unbound*, and *Poetry Unbound: 50 Poems to Open Your World* (W.W. Norton). She is the director of WWS and teaches with Antioch University, MFA and UCLA Extension.

Sharnell Blevins work spans various genres. Her play *Dreams on a Dime* was a semi-finalist in the SheLA/SheNYC Play Festival and read at the San Diego Repertory's Kuumba Fest; her story "COVID Prisms" was read during The Billie Holiday Theatre's Love in the Time of Corona, 50in50. Her poems, "Ruling" and "preparations" are found in *IO Literary Journal* inaugural edition. Sharnell's MFA is from Mount Saint Mary's University. She is a member of the AWP, Dramatist Guild, Kite City Playwrights, New Play Exchange, Playwright's Center, and Women Who Submit. Sharnell Blevins lives in the Los Angeles area with her family.

Kelly Bowen (she/her/hers) is a longtime musician turned writer. Her penchant for the stage evolved to performing stories, which spawned publications: speculative fiction - *Bards and Sages Quarterly*; memoir - "So Say We All's The Whole Alphabet;" poetry - *A Year in Ink, Volume 15*, Poet's *Underground Volume One and Fuck Isolation* and the *San Diego Poetry Annual (2020-2021 & 2022-2023).* Her friends call her relentless: in addition to writing short stories (fiction and memoir), she's writing poetry, pitching her first novel, writing the second, and in her spare time, throwing pottery and teaching yoga. Kellybowenarts.com.

Marie Cartier, an award-winning writer, received the Emerging Writers Award at the Literary Women Conference 2022. Her story "Beyond Desire: Working it Out" earned her the 2021 Drury Award in Fiction, while "Yes" received an Honorable Mention in the 2021 Roswell Award's Women Hold Up Half the Sky category. Marie's work has been recognized by the City of West Hollywood, and she has published poetry in *SAGA* and *Sinister Wisdom*, as well as short fiction on *QueerWise*. With her captivating narratives and poetic expressions, Marie Cartier has made a significant impact in the literary world.

Lisa Eve Cheby, a librarian, poet, school library advocate, and daughter of Hungarian immigrants. She holds an MFA from Antioch and an MLIS from SJSU. Her poems, essays, and reviews have appeared in journals and anthologies including *Santa Ana River Review*, *So To Speak*, *Ruminate*, *TAB*, *Drawn to Marvel*, and *Coiled Serpent*. She was writer in Residence at Sundress Academy for the Arts' Firefly Farms and Dorland Mountain Arts. Her two chapbooks are available from dancing girl press, with a third one forthcoming this Fall. http://lisacheby.wordpress.com

.CHISARAOKWU. is an Igbo-American transdisciplinary poet-artist and 2023 MacDowell Fellow. Her poetry has been supported with additional fellowships from Anaphora Arts, Brooklyn Poets, Cave Canem, and the Periplus Collective. She is also an alumna of the 2022 Tin House Winter Workshop. Her work appears in *Hayden's Ferry Review, Obsidian, Cutthroat, Cider Press Review, The Washington Post*, and more. Her poetry excavates spiritual, oral, and print archives of West Africa and its diaspora to reveal its rituals, traumas, and joy. She is also the founder of The JOY+WELL, a creative arts platform supporting African-descended women in finding their joy.

Ching-In Chen is the author of *The Heart's Traffic*; *recombinant* (2018 Lambda Literary Award for Transgender Poetry); and *how to make black paper sing* and 'Kundiman for Kin: Information Retrieval for Monsters' (Leslie Scalapino Finalist). Chen is also co-editor of *The Revolution Starts at Home: Confronting Intimate Violence Within Activist Communities* and *Here Is a Pen: an Anthology of West Coast Kundiman Poets*. They have received fellowships from Kundiman, Lambda Literary, The Watering Hole, Can Serrat, Imagining America, the Intercultural Leadership Institute and are a part of

Macondo and Voices of Our Nations Arts Foundation writing communities. Chinginchen.com

Ashton Cynthia Clarke is a nonfiction writer and performance storyteller. She has appeared in live venues in the Los Angeles area and New York City, and virtually. Her work is published in *The Storytelling Bistro*, *Olney Magazine*, and *These Black Bodies: a Chorus of Black Voices*. Of Afro-Caribbean heritage, Ashton developed an animated short based on a family member's life in Jamaica: "Titta and the Mango." In her writing, Ashton strives to connect to ancestors and other beloveds whose ties may transcend even death. She aims to present universal sentiments that will transport her audiences along with her. Instagram: @ashton.c.clarke

Lisbeth Coiman is a bilingual author born in Venezuela. She earned her BA in Modern Languages at Universidad Metropolitana, Caracas and a Masters in Education at Northwestern Oklahoma State University. She was an adult ESL teacher for 25 years. Her first book, *I Asked the Blue Heron: A Memoir* (2017) explores the intersection between immigration and mental health. Her poetry collection, *Uprising / Alzamiento* (FLP, 2021) alerts us about democracy's fragility. An avid reader and committed literary citizen, Coiman loves reviewing books for literary journals. She has been a member of WWS since 2015. Coiman lives in Los Angeles.

Carly Marie DeMento is a poet and active citizen living in Encinitas, California. She recently began to submit her work at the age of 40. A Pushcart Prize nominee, her poems have appeared or are forthcoming in the *North American Review*, *Kestrel*, and *Green Hills Literary Lantern*. Her poem "Inheritance" was selected as a finalist for the 2023 James Hearst Poetry Prize.

Deborah Edler Brown is a poet, fiction writer, teacher, author, and performer with two poetry chapbooks, a non-fiction book, and a variety of journals and anthologies to her name. She was born in Brazil, raised in Pittsburgh, and has family on four continents. She learned to dance before she learned to walk, started writing in grade school, and is entirely in love with the magic and rhythm of words. You can find more of her work at www.DeborahEdlerBrown.com

Angela M. Franklin is an essayist, poet, teacher, visual artist, and documentarian. She is a native of Los Angeles, and holds an MFA from Antioch University Los Angeles. She is a fellow of Cave Canem, Voices of our Nation (VONA), and Hurston/Wright. She has taught high school students and incarcerated teens. Franklin's poems and essays are published in anthologies and online publications. She is completing a memoir, *Patent Leather Sundays*, and a book of poetry *Cutting Through Keloids*. Her website is angelafranklin.com.

Elizabeth Galoozis's poems have appeared in *Air/Light*, *Pidgeonholes*, *RHINO*, *Witness*, *Sinister Wisdom*, and elsewhere. She serves as a reader for *The Maine Review* and *Abandon Journal* and has been nominated for a Pushcart Prize. Elizabeth was selected by Claire Wahmanholm for AWP's Writer to Writer Program in 2022. She works as a librarian and lives in southern California. Elizabeth can be found on Twitter and Instagram at @thisamericanliz.

Anita Gill is a Fulbright Scholar whose work has appeared in *The Iowa Review*, *Kweli*, *Prairie Schooner*, *The Coachella Review*, *Los Angeles Review of Books*, *The Rumpus*, and elsewhere. Her writing has been listed as Notable in Best American Essays and has won The Iowa Review Award in Nonfiction. She holds an MA in Literature from American University, and an MFA in Writing from Pacific University. She currently serves as Nonfiction Editor for *Hypertext Review* while working on her first novel. Find her online at www.anitagill.ink.

liz gonzález is the author of *The Original OLG: San Bernardino's First Our Lady of Guadalupe Church*, forthcoming (Los Nietos Press); *Dancing in the Santa Ana Winds: Poems y Cuentos New and Selected* (Los Nietos Press, 2018); and *Beneath Bone* (Manifest Press, 2000). Her creative nonfiction and poetry recently appeared in *HTI Open Plaza*, *Air/Light*, *Poets & Writers Magazine*, *San Bernardino Singing*, and *The*

International Literary Quarterly. In 2016, she founded Women's Write Inn, a rotating group of women poets and writers who meet regularly to write and support each other. A fourth-generation Californian, liz lives in Long Beach.

Susana Gonzales was raised in the Air Force and lives in southern California with her wife Suzanne. She is an ardent feminist and is slowly exploring her Mexican American roots through her poetry. She has been published in *Sheila Na Gig, Gyroscope Review, One Art,* T*he Santa Fe Literary Review, Muddy River Poetry Review, Drunk Monkeys* and *As You Were: The Military Review.*

Toni Ann Johnson is a two-time NAACP Image Award nominee for Outstanding Literary Work, first in 2015 for her novel, *Remedy For a Broken Angel,* and again in 2023 for her linked story collection *Light Skin Gone to Waste,* which won the Flannery O'Connor Award. A novella, *Homegoing,* published in 2021, is a sequel to *Light Skin Gone to Waste* and won Accents Publishing's inaugural novella contest. She's been a Sundance Screenwriter's Lab fellow, a Callaloo Writer's Workshop fellow, and a Hurston/Wright fellow. She lives in Los Angeles and is proud to be a Women Who Submit board member.

Bonnie S. Kaplan (she/her) is a poet and educator. Her work has appeared in numerous anthologies and journals, most recently in *Sinister Wisdom, Room,* and *The Bellevue Literary Review,* where her poem, "Mastectomy, Simple," was a finalist for the 2021 Marica and Jan Vilcek Poetry Prize. bonnieskaplan.com

Shelly Holder is a poet, book club and workshop facilitator who is working on founding a library of literary magazines. Her poetry can be found (in print and/or audio) in literary magazines such as *Iron Horse Literary Review, One Art,* and *Gyroscope Review,* and floating around Youtube through various poetry channels. You can follow up by visiting www.shellyholder.com or her Facebook profile /shellyholderpoet. Shelly lives in the San Gabriel Valley, where she is a proud new chapter lead for Women Who Submit and also struggles to get an orange tree to fruit.

Hazel Kight Witham is a mother, writer, teacher, artist, and slam coach who leads workshops on building a sustainable teaching practice. Her poetry, memoir, fiction, and interviews can be found in *The Sun*, *Bellevue Literary Review*, *Made in L.A. Vol.4*, *Mutha Magazine*, *Integrated Schools*, *United Teacher*, *Cultural Weekly*, and *Rising Phoenix Review*. Hazel's work explores issues of wellness, mental health, social justice and peace-making. She is deeply grateful to WWS for helping her sustain a writing life during the wilderness of pando.

Elline Lipkin is a poet and academic. Her first book, *The Errant Thread*, was chosen by Eavan Boland for the Kore Press First Book Award. Her second, *Girls' Studies*, was published by Seal Press. Her poetry has been published in many contemporary journals and she has been in residence at Yaddo, the Virginia Center for the Creative Arts, the Dorland Mountain Arts Colony and Yefe Nof. She teaches writing workshops and is currently a Research Scholar with UCLA's Center for the Study of Women. From 2016-2018, she served as Poet Laureate of Altadena and co-edited the *Altadena Poetry Review*.

Roberta H. Martínez is an actor, director, dramaturge, playwright, and historian, with deep roots in East LA. Her produced plays: *EL ARROYO* (Eng) - Short+Sweet Hollywood; *EL ARROYO* (Eng, Esp), *XOCHIMILCO BAKERY No. 3* (Eng) Frida Kahlo Theater; *LA VENTURA* (full-length, Semi-finalist New Works/Garry Marshall Theater) and ESPIE (one-act), have had staged readings at the Frida Kahlo Theater. She's a founding member of Collective Voz and The Amapola Players. Her book, *LATINOS IN PASADENA*, was released in 2009; Arcadia Publishing. She curated exhibit — Latinx Heritage in Pasadena for Pasadena City College; a visual story of migrants and immigrants from pre-statehood to today.

Juanita E. Mantz ("JEM") is a USC Law educated lawyer, podcaster, performer, and a creative nonfiction writer who has 2 books, a YA memoir titled *Tales of an Inland Empire Girl* (Los Nietos Press, Jan 2022) which is a finalist in the 2023 Latino Books to Movie Awards and a chapbook titled *Portrait of a Deputy Public Defender*, or *how I became a punk rock lawyer* (Bamboo Dart Press, Aug 2021) which was awarded a gold medal at the International Latino Book Awards for best first book, nonfiction English. She is a Macondista and a VONA alum.

Noriko Nakada is a multi-racial Asian American who creates fiction, nonfiction, poetry, and art to capture the hidden stories she has been told not to talk about. Her memoir *Through Eyes Like Mine*, was shortlisted for the 2040 Book Award. Excerpts, essays, fiction, and poetry have appeared in *Catapult*, *Meridian*, *Kartika*, *Hippocampus*, and *Linden Avenue*. She is a member of the leadership team for Women Who Submit, an organization empowering women and non-binary writers to submit their work for publication.

Ashunda Norris is a Black feminist multidisciplinary artist with creative work that encompasses film, poetry, archiving and her own theoretical frameworks. A two-time Furious Flower Poetry Prize finalist, Ashunda holds fellowships from Cave Canem, the California Arts Council, Brooklyn Poets and Starshine & Clay. Her writing has been featured or is forthcoming in *Gulf Coast*, *Obsidian*, *Taint Taint Taint*, *Root Work Journal*, *Fence* and elsewhere. Born and raised in the heart of rural, red clay Georgia, Ashunda is now a bon-afide citified bitch living and creating in Los Angeles. Learn more at ashunda.com.

Thea Pueschel is a writer, artist, and blog managing editor for the literary nonprofit Women Who Submit, a facilitator for Shut Up & Write, and a repeated Dorland Arts Colony Resident. Thea has been published in *Short Edition*, *Perhappened*, and the *Made in L.A. Anthology: Vantage Points Volume 5*, among others.

Ramona Reeves won the 2022 Drue Heinz Literature Prize for her interconnected short story collection, *It Falls Gently All Around* *and Other Stories*, published by University of Pittsburgh Press. The collection also won the 2023 Sergio Troncoso Award for Best First Book of Fiction from the Texas Institute of Letters. Her fiction and nonfiction have appeared in New South's Micro Series, The Southampton Review, Pembroke, Bayou Magazine, Superstition Review, Texas Highways, and others. More information about her can be found at www.ramonareeves.com.

Carla Rachel Sameth is the Co-Poet Laureate for Altadena, CA. Her chapbook, *What Is Left* was published December 2021; her memoir, *One Day on the Gold Line* was reissued in 2022 and her poetry collection, *Secondary Inspections* will be released November 2023. Her writing appears in a variety of publications and has been selected three times as Notable Essays of the Year in Best American Essays. A Pushcart and Best of the Net nominee. a Pasadena Rose Poet, a West Hollywood Pride Poet, and a former PEN Teaching Artist, Carla teaches creative writing to a diverse community.

Timea Sipos is a Hungarian American writer and translator with an MFA in Creative Writing from the University of Nevada, Las Vegas. A 2021-2022 Steinbeck Fellow and winner of the Tennessee Williams & New Orleans Literary Festival Fiction Contest, her work has received support from MacDowell, the Vermont Studio Center, Tin House, Bread Loaf, the American Literary Translators Association, the Nevada Arts Council, the Black Mountain Institute, Nevada Humanities, and PEN America, among others. Her writing appears in *Prairie Schooner, Passages North, Juked, The Florida Review, Joyland,* and elsewhere. Learn more about her at www.timeasipos.com.

Saba Waheed's work has appeared in *Water~Stone Review* (Fiction Prize winner), the *Southeast Review* (Pushcart-nominated), *Bellingham Review, Lunch Ticket, Cosmonauts Avenue, Hyphen Magazine,* and others. She was a Caldera 2020 artist-in-residence. She co-produces the podcast Re:work Radio, winner of a Gracies by the Alliance for Women in Media. Saba works as the research director at the UCLA Labor Center using research as a tool to elevate community stories.

Monona Wali is an award-winning novelist, short story writer and filmmaker. Her second novel *Sutra Americana* was a finalist for the 2022 New American Press contest judged by Weike Wang. Her debut novel, *My Blue Skin Lover*, won the 2015 Independent Book Publishers Gold award for multicultural fiction. Prior to writing fiction, she was a filmmaker. "Maria's Story" won a Blue Ribbon at the American Film & Video Festival, and "Grey Area" is included in the LA Rebellion, curated by the UCLA Film and Television Archives to highlight groundbreaking work done by BIPOC filmmakers in the 70's and 80's.

Sahare Wazirali (she/her) is a poet, community organizer, and research scientist. She writes about her Pakistani and Muslim roots, intergenerational wisdom, spiritual fulfillment, and building social systems that liberate us. She studied in the fields of neuroscience, as well as social inequality and health policy at the University of Texas at Austin and Tufts Medical School. She enjoys discovering new landscapes through magical realism fiction and travel. She is currently a writer for *Brown Girl Magazine* and an Adjunct Professor of Chemistry.

Roz Weisberg is a recovering film producer who went back to school and received her MFA at Antioch University, Los Angeles in fiction. She's been published in *Bangalore Review, Manifest-Station* and *Drunk Monkey* and attended The Disquiet Writing Workshop in Lisbon, Portugal. She teaches screenwriting at UCLA Extension, is a writing specialist at Antioch, and privately coaches and edits writers working on long and short form in fiction, CNF and screenplays. When not working or writing she is planning her next adventure while awaiting March Madness.

Aruni Wijesinghe is a project manager, ESL teacher, erstwhile belly dance instructor and occasional sous chef. A Pushcart Prize and Best of the Net nominee, she has been published nationally and internationally. Her debut collection, *2 Revere Place*, is a love letter to her family and miraculous childhood in New York. Her latest collection,

The Litany of Missing (Arroyo Seco Press) is a meditation on loss, longing and love. You can follow her at www.aruniwrites.com.

Nancy Lynée Woo is a poet, writer, organizer, and climate activist who harbors a wild love for the natural world. Her debut poetry collection is *I'd Rather Be Lightning* (GASHER Press, March 2023). Nancy has received fellowships from Artists at Work, PEN America, Arts Council for Long Beach, and Idyllwild Writers Week. She holds an MFA in creative writing from Antioch University.

Dilys Wyndham Thomas (she/her/hers) grew up in Belgium and Saudi Arabia. studied in France and has since lived in Germany, Jordan, the UK and The Netherlands. Like so many others, she rediscovered writing during the pandemic lockdowns and began submitting her work in 2021. Since then, her poems and short stories have appeared in publications such as *Beyond Words, Prometheus Dreaming, Rust and Moth* and *Wild Roof Journal.* Dilys also volunteers as an assistant poetry editor at *Passengers Journal* and hosts feedback groups for Strange Birds Migratory Writing Collective. Find her online at dilyswt.com.

Sandy Yang's fiction has appeared in *Santa Monica Review, Salt Hill Journal, Juked* and elsewhere. Her story collection was named a semi-finalist for the Iowa Short Fiction Award, and she is the recipient of a Tennessee Williams Scholarship to the Sewanee Writers' Conference. She holds an MFA in fiction from the University of Arizona.

Suhasini Yeeda (she/her) is a first-generation queer Indian American from Dallas, Texas. Her work appears or is forthcoming at *Ms. Magazine, The Los Angeles Review of Books, The Indian Review, Madcap Review, Packingtown Review,* and the *Arroyo Seco Press Anthology Redshift 5.* She is a two-time Pushcart Prize nominee and a one-time nominee for The Best American Short Stories and Best of the Net. She holds her MFA in writing from Sarah Lawrence College and a BA from Texas Wesleyan University. She is the owner at NITI Communications, a small business dedicated to uplifting QTBIPOC smalls businesses and individuals.

Los Angeles native **Désirée Zamorano** is the author of the highly acclaimed literary novel, *The Amado Women*. Her novel, *Human Cargo*, was Latinidad's mystery pick of the year. An award-winning and Pushcart prize nominee short story writer her work is often an exploration of issues of invisibility, injustice or inequity. A selection of her writing can be found in *Catapult*, *Cultural Weekly*, *The Kenyon Review Online* and *Akashic's South Central Noir*. "Caperucita Roja" was chosen as a distinguished short story in Best of American Mystery and Suspense, 2022. Her historical novel *Dispossessed* is forthcoming from Rize.

Tamara Zook has over 40 years of experience in the storytelling industry as an actor and producer. Her professional acting training and experience have led to performances of new and classical works through the United States and Canada. Her extensive communication, organization, and management skills, combined with her undergraduate degree in Speech and Communication Studies and her Master of Fine Arts, provide the foundations for her work as a storyteller. As an actor/writer, she has been a finalist for Center Theatre Group's Sherwood Award and looks forward to further widening her creative world.

EDITORS

Managing Editor (poetry) **Noriko Nakada** is a member of the leadership team for Women Who Submit. A multi-racial Asian American, she creates fiction, nonfiction, poetry, and art to capture the hidden stories she has been told not to talk about. Publications include her memoir series: *Through Eyes Like Mine, Overdue Apologies,* and *I Tried. Through Eyes Like Mine* was shortlisted for the 2040 Book Award. Excerpts, essays, fiction, and poetry have appeared in *Catapult, Meridian, Kartika, Hippocampus,* and *Rising Phoenix Review.* Noriko is represented by Emily Keyes of Keyes Agency.

Managing Editor (fiction and creative nonfiction) **Ryane Nicole Granados** is the Chapters Director for Women Who Submit. She is also a Los Angeles native whose writing finds its roots in her love of community and her belief that Black motherhood is an act of social justice. Named the 2021 Established Writer and Individual Arts Fellow by the California Arts Council, her work has been featured in various publications including *Pangyrus, High Country News, The Atticus Review, Made in L.A.* and *LA Parent Magazine.* Her storytelling has also been nominated for a Pushcart Prize and showcased in KPCC's live series Unheard LA.

Fiction Editor **Lorinda Toledo** (she/her) has been an editor for *Witness, Lunch Ticket,* and *Gathering: A Women Who Submit Anthology.* Her novel-in-progress was named first runner-up for the 2019 James Jones First Novel Fellowship. Her stories have been published in the *Mississippi Review, The Normal School,* and elsewhere. She earned a PhD in literature and creative writing from the University of Nevada, Las Vegas, where she was a Barrick Graduate Fellow and a Black Mountain Institute PhD Fellow; she holds an MFA from

Antioch University Los Angeles and attended the Community of Writers Summer Fiction Workshop as an Ancinas Scholar.

Fiction Editor **Erin Anadkat** received her MFA in Creative Writing from Antioch University, Los Angeles and a B.S. in News-Editorial Journalism from University of Illinois at Champaign-Urbana. She is working on her first novel, which is about the manufacturing of culture, psychology of mixed-race identity, and self-created mythologies. Erin has attended workshops at Lighthouse, Community of Writers, and Lidia Yuknavitch's Corporeal Writing. She is co-founder of a social media agency/production company in Los Angeles, kissd, working with brands including Honda, Acura, and American Express.

Creative Nonfiction Editor **Flint** is a queer writer with a keen interest in hybridity, generative genre tampering and upsetting the applecart of heteronormative discourse about sex/uality. A 2022 Lambda Literary Nonfiction Fellow, Flint earned an MFA in Writing from the School of Critical Studies at CalArts, and her work has appeared in *The Offing, Arts & Letters* (Unclassifiable Contest winner), *Erotic Review, NAILED Magazine*, and *Staging Social Justice*, among other publications and anthologies.

Creative Nonfiction Editor **Laura Sturza** is co-host of the WWS Saturday check-in. She is a writer/teacher living in Rockville, Maryland, after 20 years in L.A.—her other home. Her creative nonfiction is published in *The LA Times, Lunch Ticket, The Washington Post,* and *Shondaland,* among others. She wrote, produced, and starred in the one-woman show, *Finding the Perfect Place to Live in 111 Gyrations.* Laura is completing the memoir, *The Adventures of an Almost 50, Never Married, Wannabe-Wife.* She was a graduate advisor at the University of Southern California and received an MA in Communications/Writing/Theatre from George Mason University.

Poetry Editor **Hazel Kight Witham** is a mother, writer, teacher, slam coach, and artist who leads workshops on building a sustainable teaching practice. Her poetry, memoir, fiction, and interviews can be found in *The Sun, Bellevue Literary Review, Made in L.A. Vol.4, Mutha Magazine, Integrated Schools, United Teacher, Cultural Weekly,* and *Rising Phoenix Review*. Hazel's work explores issues of wellness, mental health, healing, social justice and peace-making. She earned a BA from Brown University and an M.F.A. in Creative Writing from Antioch University Los Angeles and has been a proud member of Women Who Submit since 2016.

Poetry Editor **Luivette Resto** is on the Board for Women Who Submit. She is an award-winning poet, a mother of three revolutionary humans, a Wonder Woman fan, and a middle school English teacher. She is a CantoMundo and Macondo Fellow and a Pushcart Prize nominee. Her two books of poetry *Unfinished Portrait* and *Ascension* have been published by Tía Chucha Press. Her third poetry collection *Living on Islands Not Found on Maps,* published by FlowerSong Press, won silver for the 2022 Juan Felipe Herrera Best Poetry Book Award at the International Latino Book Awards.

Poetry Editor **Aruni Wijesinghe** joined Women Who Submit in 2018. She is a project manager, ESL teacher, erstwhile belly dance instructor and occasional sous chef. She holds a BA in English, an AA in dance, and a certification in TESOL. A Pushcart Prize and Best of the Net nominee, her work has been published both nationally and internationally. Her debut collection, *2 Revere Place,* is a love letter to her family and miraculous childhood in New York. Her latest collection, *The Litany of Missing,* is a meditation on loss, longing and love.

Drama Editor **Lucy Rodriguez-Hanley** (she/her/ella) is the Chapters Liaison for Women Who Submit and Long Beach, CA Chapter Lead. She creates engaging stories for and about bilingual, bicultural brown girls and women. Her writing is featured in *The Latinx Project at NYU* and HarperVia's *Somewhere We Are Human* edited by Reyna Grande and Sonia Guiñansaca. She has been awarded fellowships from Tin House, Macondo and VONA. Her film, *The Big Deal,* won the Imagen Award for Best Theatrical Short and was screened at festivals throughout the US. A Dominicana via Washington Heights, she lives in Long Beach, CA with her husband and two children.

Advising Editor **Tisha Marie Reichle-Aguilera** (she/her) has presented on submission strategies at Macondo Writers Workshop, the Latina Writers Conference, and various colleges/universities. A Chicana Feminist and former Rodeo Queen, she writes so the desert landscape of her childhood can be heard as loudly as the urban chaos of her adulthood. She is obsessed with food. A former high school teacher, she earned an MFA at Antioch University Los Angeles and a PhD at University of Southern California. Her fiction has been nominated for a Pushcart Prize, Best of the Net, Best Microfiction, and is spotlighted in *Best Small Fictions 2022.* Her short stories have been anthologized in *Rural Writers of Color* (EastOver Press 2023), *Made in L.A.* Volume 4 and 5 (Resonant Earth 2022 and 2023), and *Puro Chicanx Writers of the 21st Century.* Her play, *Blind Thrust Fault,* was featured in Center Theater Group Writers' Workshop Festival. Her YA novel, *Breaking Pattern (Inlandia Books 2023),* is about a girl who loves horses more than people and competes in junior rodeo in Riverside, CA.

TEAM

Xochitl-Julisa Bermejo, *Co-founder/Executive Director*
Alyss Dixson, *Cofounder/Advisor*
Tisha Marie Reichle-Aguilera, *Anthology Advisor*
Lauren Eggert-Crowe, *Special Events Coordinator*
Cybele Garcia Kohel, *Fundraising Coordinator*
Noriko Nakada, *Anthology Co-Managing Editor*
Ryane Nicole Granados, *Chapters Director & Anthology Co-Managing Editor*
Lucy Rodriguez-Hanley, *Chapters Liaison & Long Beach Chapter Lead*
Sakae Manning, *Submit One Coordinator*
Thea Pueschel, *Blog Managing Editor*
Ashton Cynthia Clarke, *Social Media Editor*
Shipra Agarwal, *Website Manager*

BOARD

Board President, Xochitl-Julisa Bermejo
Board Treasurer, Lauren Eggert-Crowe
Board Secretary, Kate Maruyama
Jessica Ceballos y Campbell
Melissa Chadburn
Toni Ann Johnson
Luivette Resto
Rachelle Yousuf
Désirée Zamorano

FOUNDERS

Alyss Dixson
Dr. Ashaki M. Jackson
Xochitl-Julisa Bermejo

ABOUT THE ORGANIZATION

Women Who Submit seeks to empower women and nonbinary writers by creating physical and virtual spaces for sharing information to support and encourage submissions to literary journals, fellowships, and residencies. We promote our mission, future projects, and public events through our social media channels. Membership is free.

After 10+ years of working and growing with Avenue 50 as our fiscal sponsor, Women Who Submit became a 501(c)(3)!

Donate to WWS

CORE VALUES

Generosity - WWS was founded as a free and open space for sharing.

Shared Leadership - WWS is an egalitarian community.

Inclusion & Accessibility - WWS fights for gender parity and diverse representation in publishing by serving women and non-binary writers, including trans women, woman-identifying, and genderqueer individuals.

Resilience - WWS celebrates submissions, acceptances, and rejections equally.

To find a chapter in your area or for information about how to create a Women Who Submit chapter in your area, visit the **Join Us** page on our website: womenwhosubmitlit.org

CONTACT US

womensubmit@gmail.com

FOLLOW US

Twitter/Instagram @WomenWhoSubmit
facebook.com/women who submit
YouTube @womenwhosubmitlosangeles2626

www.ingramcontent.com/pod-product-compliance
Lightning Source LLC
Chambersburg PA
CBHW061259210726
48293CB00003B/1030

* 9 7 8 1 9 5 4 9 0 1 9 1 9 *